Making a Bad Situation Good

To: Grace:

As a teacher, you are making a positive difference for young people. You are making many good situations better! May you always be blessed with joy and good health.

Raj le Chopra

MAKING A BAD SITUATION

Good

by Raj K. Chopra

Thomas Nelson Publishers
Nashville • Camden • New York

Dedicated to my
grandmother
who made me
believe
I was "somebody"
and to
people
whose generosity and support
continue to inspire me to
believe
in the vitality of
the American dream

Contents

Acknowledgments

I received the inspiration for writing this book from many people. This motivation came in the form of telephone calls, letters, and face to face conversations after I spoke to various organizations and groups. A letter from Kate Gray, a first-grade teacher in the Shawnee Mission School District, provided the final push when she wrote,

> I am a first grade teacher and enjoyed hearing you speak to our PTA group a couple of weeks ago. Your thoughts and philosophy on education and 'life' in general are inspirational. Have you ever considered writing your ideas in a booklet to distribute among the district PTA groups, etc.? A booklet of this description would be worthwhile and your messages would reach more people.

To all those people who supported my efforts, I owe thanks.

I am indebted to Dr. J. Fred Parker for his invaluable editorial assistance and insightful comments. I also extend appreciation to Jean Younger for her help.

My sincere appreciation goes to a number of people whose sense of generosity and helping attitude not only enriched my life but also provided the momentum to achieve my goals. Professors David Elsass, Willard Fox, Samuel Cooper, Robert Keefe, Leslie Chamberlin, William York, Russell Coffey, Neil Pohlmann, Morris Weinberger, Malcolm Campbell, Gary Hess, and other officials at Bowling Green State University provided me the support and educational stimulation to launch a successful career in public schools administration.

I am grateful to both Craig Gifford, executive director,

and Ann Fauley of Ohio School Boards Association for their encouragement and support. I also extend appreciation to Dr. Victor Cottrell for his confidence in me. To John Kaczenski, under whom I did my administrative internship and who later helped me gain invaluable administrative experience, I express my gratitude and appreciation for his support and stimulation.

I owe a debt of gratitude to Lakota Board of Education, Rising Sun, Ohio, and Perkins Board of Education, Sandusky, Ohio, for allowing me the opportunity to associate with their school systems. I commend Leonard Morse, Ralph Waite, and other members of the Medina Board of Education, Medina, Ohio, for their support and confidence. To the Bellefontaine Board of Education members Bill Troop, Joan Kelly, Marilyn Miller, Olga Henry, Dean Hess, and Lester Cerwinsky go my praise and respect for giving me my first chance as the superintendent of a school system. Their trust continues to inspire me to give my best in serving young people and communities.

I am, of course, appreciative of Council Bluffs School Board members John Moats, Sam Brown, Ken Petersen, Virdus Alton, John Luther, Dr. Eugene Marsh, Mike Winchester, Stan Robertson, Rich Stoufer, Joanne Carrithers, Bob Hegland, Jackie McLellan, Bill Cutler, Bob Nelson, and Kevin Monroe for making me a part of their team to achieve the goals and improve the image of the school system. I also thank Council Bluffs citizens for their active participation, enthusiastic support, and dedicated involvement that produced positive results in their schools.

I am grateful to Mrs. Catherine A. Slipper for her love and kindness.

I am indeed grateful to the Shawnee Mission, Kansas, School Board members Joan Bowman, Tom Rawlings,

Ann Burns, Ken Bayer, Laura Hendricks, Don Culp, the late Cynthia O'Connell, Dick Spears, Julie Miller, and Ruth Roudebush for their support and confidence.

My highest praises go to teachers and other staff members and administrators in all the school districts I served, for their support and cooperation without which progress and success would not have been possible. I especially acknowledge my colleagues Joe Scalzo, Jim Howard, Ray Newberg, Carm Gioiello, Tom Kenny, Ted Stilwill, and others for their dedication that produced the big turnaround in Council Bluffs. I also extend appreciation to my colleagues in the Shawnee Mission School District for their support and cooperation in meeting the challenges before them.

I express my gratitude to my wife Sue and our children, Dick, Lucky, and Komal, for their love and support. Sue served as a loving critic and encouraging partner in discussing ideas and generating thoughts during the writing of the book. Dick, Lucky, and Komal assumed complete responsibility for typing and retyping the manuscript. Their diligence and patience enabled us to meet all the deadlines. Their performance was outstanding, and they did it with pride. It turned out to be a family project in which we all played an important part in seeing it to completion.

To have the opportunity of serving and inspiring students and teachers and of making them feel special is a gift of God for which I give thanks.

RAJ K. CHOPRA

Part I

The Possibilities

1

Thinking Realistically

When my wife Sue saw me carrying the big suit-case up our walk, she stared at it in dismay. "Why are you bringing that back?" she asked.

"Give me the rest of the day to tell you," I groaned. "It's been an awful trip."

Three days earlier I had left for Council Bluffs, Iowa, where I had been offered the post of school superintend-ent. On this brief visit I was to meet with the board to learn about my new responsibilities and to find out more about the community in which my wife, our three chil-dren, and I would live.

For the previous two years I had been school superin-tendent in Bellefontaine, Ohio, and though we were very happy there, the Council Bluffs invitation offered an unusual challenge. Not only was it a much larger dis-trict with twenty-two elementary, five junior high, and two high schools but also its school board publicly ad-mitted to having serious problems.

Problems have always fascinated me. I believe that practically any difficulty can be overcome, even turned into an asset, if we carefully explore our options, think realistically, and act decisively. I am called a "realistic thinker," and I am proud of that. These principles of realistic thinking work!

Sue also thinks in practical terms. In fact she had suggested, as I got ready to leave on that short indoctrination trip, that I take our largest suitcase packed full of clothes. "Leave it in Council Bluffs, Raj," she had said. "It will be something we won't have to move later."

Now, after three days, I was back home lugging the same suitcase, telling Sue I had changed my mind about moving. She had started to prepare the family dinner, so I slumped down at the kitchen table and began to describe what had happened to me.

"Remember that CBS '60 Minutes' television report on the Council Bluffs schools we saw two years ago? Mike Wallace pointed out that student test scores there were the lowest in all of Iowa. Remember what he said about how run-down the school system was, with a board of education embroiled in internal strife, and how this was reflected in factionalism and polarization of the community? Well, unfortunately it's all true—even worse!"

"Yes, I remember," Sue said, "but wasn't that one of the things that challenged you about the job?"

"Well, yes," I sighed, "but why try to take on a hopeless task like that? I'm not sure how I could help them solve their problems. It's a 'no win' situation."

I told her about my opening encounter with the motel clerk. Recognizing my name on the register from news reports on the prospective new superintendent, she had muttered sardonically, "Good luck; you'll need it." Then she went on to tell me about irate parents, school board meetings exploding into shouting matches, and demoralized teachers fleeing to other jobs.

But it wasn't just the school system that seemed to be in trouble. I had quickly sensed something wrong about the general attitude of the community. I told Sue how I had walked about the city itself, talking with people in shopping centers, banks, and restaurants and visiting them in their homes.

"Maybe they're still smarting from that television report," I said, "but everyone I met seems to be suffering from a horrible self-image. Hardly anyone had anything good to say about the schools. Many advised me bluntly not to take the job. It seems as though a dark pall, a gloom cloud, has settled over the people.

"The man who got to me most and whose comments seemed to sum up all the rest was sitting on his front doorstep in his undershirt, drinking a can of beer, when I came by on my way to an elementary school right next door. I asked him what he thought about his community's public education system.

"He stared at me for a moment. Then he lowered his beer can and turned toward the school. 'If that place was on fire, I wouldn't throw a drop of water on it!'

"After that," I said, going over to the sink to wash my hands, "it seemed I couldn't get home fast enough. I'd better look elsewhere."

Later at the dinner table I explained everything to our sons, thirteen-year-old Dick and ten-year-old Lucky, and to our seven-year-old daughter, Komal.

"There's just no hope for that place," I concluded. "I'm better off here."

The table was quiet for a moment. Then Dick spoke up, "But, Dad, what about your faith? You're always telling us how the Lord can turn problems into opportunities."

I could not answer him for a moment. He had thrown my own words back at me. I made a feeble effort to respond and let it go at that. That night I went to bed early but could not sleep for quite a while. What really had happened to my faith? My sense of seeing life as a challenge? The more I thought about it, the more convinced I became that Dick's question was valid.[1]

The difficulty I was having in coming to grips with the challenge was basically due to fear. Admitting that, I began to pray. How long I lay there praying I do not know, but when I turned on my bedside lamp to see the clock, it was 2:30 A.M.

Sue was awakened by the light and sleepily asked, "What is the matter?" Rather than answering, I grabbed her hand and made her touch my face, which was wet with tears. Then fully awake, she repeated her question. I told her the weird but vivid dream from which I had just awakened. Its climaxing words, "I will help you," were still ringing in my ears.

I saw myself in a land where there were many flat-topped mud houses. People wearing long robes were gathered in a huge open space. I heard hymns being sung. I found myself in front of a small house where stood a tall gentleman with a flowing beard and an all white robe. I asked him if there was a microphone around so that I could make an announcement to all the people gathered there. He said that the microphone was on the roof.

I thanked him and climbed the old wooden ladder leaning against the wall. Reaching the roof, I looked around but was unable to find the microphone.

I climbed back down and was about to leave when I met the white-robed man again. "Did you find the microphone?" he asked.

No was my answer.

He gave me specific directions to go up and look for a golden microphone in the right corner of the rooftop. Again I started up the old wooden ladder, but it was shaking so much that I felt insecure and backed down. I went around to the side of the house and found a ramp.

As I reached the top of the ramp, the edge of the roof changed to the form of a big, black beast that began to violently shake the building and tried to push me over the side into a deep, dark valley below. The beast had two large shining horns. In an effort to maintain my balance, I reached out to grab those steellike horns. The animal was shaking its head ferociously, but I was able to hang on to its horns. I struggled to climb on the back of the animal but had no success. As I looked down into the valley that was waiting to swallow me in its unknown depths, I continued my struggle.

Suddenly I felt a strong arm around me, and I heard the words "I will help you." The reassuring words and the touch of that enfolding arm dissolved the fear within me. I found myself up on the roof with the golden microphone in the right-hand corner just as I had been told.

With that I awoke. Were the words "I will help you" to be taken as divine direction? Was the exercise of faith that Dick had talked about the previous evening being reaffirmed through this dream, of all things?

As I continued to seek God's will, I found myself at peace about the new opportunity. I did not unpack that big suitcase. Four weeks later it went along with us as we moved to Council Bluffs.

2

Hats Off to Council Bluffs

W hen we arrived in Council Bluffs in August 1978, I was somewhat apprehensive about the task ahead but excited too. I had to view it as another step along the path of my professional advancement that we set out to accomplish when we first came to the United States in 1969.

I had been a teacher for six years. Then, principalships in the Lakota School District in Rising Sun, Ohio, and the Perkins School District in Sandusky, Ohio, were the next steps toward my appointment in 1973 as assistant superintendent of the Medina City Schools, Medina, Ohio. My primary goal to become superintendent of a school district was achieved in June 1976 when I signed a contract with the Bellefontaine, Ohio, Board of Education.

The consultant hired by the Council Bluffs School Board to assist in the search process for a superintendent described in his report the problem I now faced: "The situation in Council Bluffs is one of disarray and disunity. Many people have lost faith in the quality of their schools, in the quality of teaching, and indeed have lost faith in themselves."

The board of education had accepted the resignation of the superintendent of schools in February 1978. The mistrust, or at least lack of trust, among administrators, board members, teachers, and the community resulted in the appointment of three administrators to manage the district as a triumvirate while the board began the search for a new superintendent. Anyone involved in decision making knows that it is virtually impossible for three people who possess equal authority to make workable decisions.

To confuse matters even more, all three administrators were also applicants for the superintendent position. One of them later jokingly told me that the three of them were racing each day to park in the superintendent's parking place and more than once came close to colliding with each other. This lack of coordination of human resources was symptomatic of the poor relationships within the school system. Internal and external communication seemed to be at the lowest possible level.

As I met with the board of education that very first evening, I listened carefully as they outlined the problems as they perceived them. They talked about the new group called "PIN" (Parents Information Network), which had been established at the board's insistence to open channels of communication with parents and thus to regain their support and confidence. It was the only bright spot in the whole sordid picture. The majority of the board members had very definite ideas about what they thought needed to be done. Their voiced concerns focused on

- loss of central office leadership
- lack of public confidence
- poor test scores and the need for emphasis on basic skills

- ineffective curriculum
- communication gap between the board and the community
- loss of vision in the educational community itself
- lack of prioritizing financial resources
- community and board belief that the district had too many administrators
- an alarming lack of discipline in the schools
- futile board meetings that lasted until the "wee hours of the morning" with nothing being accomplished
- adversarial relationships resulting in overall decline

My mind went back to when Sue and I were invited to Council Bluffs to have the final consultation with the board and to meet some citizens before taking the post. It was Sue's first visit there. I assumed that the board's intention was to introduce us to as many people as possible so that they could ascertain the views of various segments of the community before making the final decision about hiring me.

An administrator drove us to the home of another board member to meet a group of citizens. Just as we got out of the car, a photographer jumped out from behind a tree to take our picture. The incident was somewhat shocking, since I had always made myself readily available to news people, and I usually enjoyed good experiences with them.

Someone later told me that the photographer had been tipped off concerning where I would be by one of the board members. It was easy to see how both the board and the school personnel had failed to maintain appropriate contact with the media. The news people had to depend on outside sources to gain inside information. I realized then that a most important task would be to build trust not only within the board but also with the news media.

When we went into the house, we found about twelve people gathered in the living room. After a few minutes of casual conversation, the host board member said, "Well, the time is here to begin the interrogation." I was puzzled at the use of the word *interrogation*. It had an ominous sound. I could not understand why a board of education would permit a candidate to be placed in such a position.

I was even more concerned about Sue who had not been in such a situation before. I wondered whether I should have brought her with me. But when I looked across at her, she seemed quite calm, which gave me additional confidence. I answered the volley of questions with candor and without fear. As I did so, I felt a sense of strength and inner peace.

Some of the questions were of the opinion type, obviously designed to determine how my ideas aligned with those of the questioner. Some questions were such that my answers might place me in conflict with particular segments of the community. I had gathered by now that the community was seriously fragmented.

I also sensed that the purpose of the group was not to discover what I would do for their youth, but rather to find reasons why I would not be a suitable candidate. The administrator who had brought us here, and who had been sitting patiently, finally spoke out and objected to both the method and the style of questioning. It was not so much *what* they asked but *how* they asked, he said. After that, the exchange took on less the form of an inquisition.

After spending another day in the city, we returned to Bellefontaine. The Monday evening the board was to take official action, I received a call from one of the board members. He advised me not to accept the job. The move would not be good for my family, he said, assuring me that he was advising me as he would advise his own son.

But, by a 5–2 vote, the board offered me a one-year contract. I had verbally accepted the offer and went back to Council Bluffs for a three-day visit, this time to do my own walking and talking with various people in the community. My previous visits had been planned and controlled by the board of education. (It was on this trip that I took along the suitcase I would supposedly leave in Council Bluffs.) Despite much advice to the contrary, I eventually signed the contract.

The Monumental Problems

How does one go about making a bad situation like this one into something good?

I recognized my initial task was to create a climate of understanding that would lead to trust, pride, and a unity of purpose. In order to accomplish this, I had first to reach out and articulate to the community what was right with their school system. We needed to assess our resources and build on the existing strengths. I discovered that the visit to Council Bluffs by the crew of CBS's "60 Minutes" had made the bad situation even worse. It had further contributed to the erosion of the self-confidence of the Council Bluffs people.

I found that an unusually large number of the citizenry were good, dedicated people genuinely interested in good education for all children. I *liked* the Council Bluffs people. The clear need was to give a personal touch to communication, so I made myself available to any group or organization that wanted me to speak to them or listen to their ideas and concerns.

One of my first efforts to communicate was with a group made up primarily of minority parents who were quite angry about the lack of responsiveness on the part of the school district administration. I arrived at the meeting place about 7:00 P.M., accompanied by the president and vice-president of the board. This was obviously the group's first opportunity to express their anger and frustration in such a forum. They had plenty of ammunition, and I became an excellent target. After their anger was vented somewhat through the open interaction, they agreed with my suggestion to actively assist in helping to solve the problems. Subsequently, that group became one of the biggest supporters of the school district.

My second meeting was with parents of students with learning and physical disabilities. They were annoyed—even a bit hostile—and wanted some action. The newly hired director of special education was with me to absorb the full blast from this group. We pledged to work with them and invited them to be involved in seeking a solution.

The lack of central office leadership had created a serious vacuum of direction, authority, and responsibility. Teachers found limited support to help them carry out their duties. The central office, engulfed in its own controversies with the board and the community, had no time to serve in a support-and-service role to the staff. Teachers wanted someone, in addition to their school principals, to be available to listen to their concerns. They had a sense of being forgotten and ignored. Educational innovations such as open spaces, nongraded schools, and individual-guided education were being introduced in the school district without consulting teachers or principals. Some of the teachers assigned to

[17]

open-space schools were neither comfortable nor compatible with this style of instruction.

All these factors led to staff frustration and low morale. The apparent lack of control was also affecting their attitudes. They perceived their emotional needs in such a stressful situation to be unmet.

The conflict among board members and the lack of effective leadership from the central office, coupled with the teachers' frustration, were taking their toll on student achievement which was, in turn, leading to unhappiness among parents. The school principals were doing their own thing in an effort to at least have some order and direction in their respective buildings. A by-product of this confusion was a mounting discipline problem.

Items needing repair in the school buildings, such as chipped plaster and faulty plumbing, were taking weeks and months to be corrected—and sometimes were never fixed. The school yards were not properly maintained, either.

Central office administrators were generally suspicious that someone from among their own number was plotting against them, ready to stab them in the back. This lack of trust resulted in poorly coordinated efforts to maximize the use of staff talent and financial resources.

All in all, it seemed that everyone had lost heart. I realized that a firm, positive approach to these incredible problems was needed. I drew up this agenda, which can be used as a model in making any bad situation good.

    1.   Create a climate of *listening*.

    2.   *Communicate aggressively* with any and every group, and do so with a personal touch.

    3.   *Expect administrators to be responsive to parents' concerns.* Administrators were to respond to such concerns within twenty-four hours of receiving the complaint.

4. *Relate to the community* to alter existing perception problems and create new lines of communication.

5. *Solicit every citizen's help* not only in identifying problems but also in finding solutions.

6. *Establish an immediate open-door policy* toward students, teachers, and citizens.

7. *Visit the classes* in order to become acquainted with teachers and students alike.

8. Promise there will be *no secrets and no surprises.*

9. *Establish goals and demand accountability.*

10. Work with those administrators who have high personal goals and *build a team* of those who will make things happen. Teamwork leads to better performances.

The Big Turnaround

After I had a brainstorming session with teachers and administrators, the idea of pride emerged as a rallying point to bring people together. This resulted in the birth of "Pride Week," which since 1979 has become an annual, areawide celebration.

To promote this newly generated idea, I personally went to community leaders, one at a time, to present the concept and seek their acceptance and support. This strategy worked. The city council, the chamber of commerce, churches, civic and service clubs, neighborhood groups, professional organizations, even senior citizens with no direct involvement with schools, made a commitment to this idea. They believed that the time was ripe for all of us to shed old complexes and forge ahead with unity for a strong, vibrant community. It was, however, interesting that just as the school board had not offered me a contract by unanimous vote, neither did the celebration of Pride Week receive unanimous approval. Fortunately though, almost everyone in the community was quite excited about the idea.

My colleagues in the central office provided dynamic leadership in articulating the idea, promoting the concept, and winning the support of principals and teachers. The local parent groups from each school also played a major support role in preparing for Pride Week. District level administrators were able to demonstrate their leadership by marketing the idea and working directly with people rather than from afar.

The enthusiasm and fervor began to mount. One of the things I wanted was involvement of all segments of the community toward a common goal. The results soon became apparent. There were four hundred persons from all parts of the city serving on various committees. The traditional divisive boundary between east and west sides of the city was forgotten. Everyone worked to build a strong bridge of cooperation and understanding, and to accentuate what was good about our community. The introduction and subsequent ownership of the idea by several segments of the community and the success of Project Pride are presented in the People Power Components diagram. The role of communication from one step to the next is emphasized to ensure success for each phase.

The excitement built steadily in anticipation of the first Pride Week, April 22 to 29, 1979. The city newspaper, *Nonpareil,* announced that it would bring out a special Pride edition on April 22. Across the Missouri River, the *Omaha World Herald* also showed an extraordinary interest in our project by publishing news stories of the coming events.

The business community expressed its pride by special advertisements in the newspaper. The Great Plains Beef Company in a quarter page ad said, "Sure, we're proud...we're proud to be your city's largest employer."

PEOPLE POWER
COMPONENTS

POSITIVE PUBLIC PERCEPTION

Pride
Project

COMMUNICATION

COMMUNICATION

Perseverance

Progress

Personal perspective

Overcoming obstacles

Developing Ownership

COMMUNICATION

COMMUNICATION

Selling an idea

PEOPLE

Supporting each other

Pulling together

Praise

Partnership

Positive

Perception

Receiving support from media

PROGRESS

PRIDE

COMMUNICATION

COMMUNICATION

Press
Promotion

Advertisements from hardware stores, local hospitals, restaurants, real estate companies, banks, and automobile dealers covered page after page.

The publisher of the *Nonpareil* typified the general attitude of the community by outlining its own responsibility as the city's newspaper: "It must help promote everything it considers good in the community, and to fearlessly fight to get rid of the bad." Pride Week provided the opportunity to make the bad good and to perpetuate the good that was already there.

The die was cast. The climate was created. The attitude was developed. Enthusiasm was generated. The good and the positive in the community were beginning to unfold. Pride Week opened where it should—the first activity of the weeklong celebration was in the churches. In the sanctuaries of all faiths were expressions of thanks and prayers for strengthening the spiritual life of the community. This was the starting point to revitalize the city and help it reach new heights—to explore, to dream, and to believe what it could be.

The newspaper's banner headline reporting the event read "Pride Week: A Step Forward." The article said, "Including children and adults, well over 10,000 people were involved in the preparation for this weeklong celebration, kicked off this morning with special church services throughout Council Bluffs, Carter Lake, and Crescent."

On the final day of Pride Week, a massive crowd gathered to watch the largest parade ever held in the city. Of the 170 entries over 30 floats displayed Council Bluffs schools' commitment to excellence, including a float entered by the board of education that proclaimed their concern to provide the best educational opportunities for all students.

One float featuring a big apple was captioned "An

Apple for a Teacher." Another float declared, "Blast with Basics." Marching bands, cheerleaders, drill teams, and kids of all ages gave a visual message to spectators—Yes, Council Bluffs kids are good! Yes, they are learning in schools. Yes, our teachers are the type we can be proud of. School principals displayed their students and teachers with a clear message that every student *can* and *will* achieve.

Not only the students and teachers were showing their pride; the local businesses, the historical society, the museum, the senior citizens, the retired teachers, the neighborhood groups, and the churches joined in the effort. Each reflected on the heritage of which Council Bluffs could be proud.

David Krajicek, a reporter with the *Nonpareil,* captured the moment of pride with a story headlined: "Council Bluffs' Pride Bursts into Bloom!" The story is encouraging to read.

The trees and flowers were budding this morning. Leaves were shoving their way out of the wombs that have held them dormant all winter. So was Council Bluffs. Some say, though, that it has been enclosed in that womb much longer than just a couple of months. But at least for today, this city was awakened. You don't need to read the newspaper today to get a feel for the pride that has been displayed here for the past week. Did you see the kids in the parade, the way they stuck their chests out, bursting with pride?

This pride stuff is no farce. It has rubbed off on everyone. This morning, as floats were lining up, everyone was excited. Spectators began lining Broadway as early as 9 A.M. Some floats were in position at 8, with workers busily applying the finishing touches. They were all proud of their work. A Lewis Central Schools entry had more than 18,000 white napkins attached to it. Another, sponsored by the Fraternal Order of Latin Americans Club, featured Our Lady of Guadalupe. Many of the school floats proclaimed the pride students felt in their school, and most noted the quality education they are receiving. There were bands. There were floats from Iowa School for the Deaf, Council Bluffs Schools, St. Albert, Lewis Central, and Iowa Western Community College. There was a pontoon boat, riding on a trailer, from Carter Lake. There were cheerleaders, pompom girls, drums and horns. Thousands upon thousands of Bluffs residents applauded, they laughed, they cheered, they smiled. Senior citizens and toddlers, Boy Scouts and Camp Fire Girls, the middle-aged and the teens—everyone had a good time.

The newspaper story concluded, "The sun shone and the people of Council Bluffs beamed."[1]

Pride Week came to a close, but its memories will long stay with both observers and participants. How did it all go? And what did it leave behind?

"I was surprised how smoothly Council Bluffs' Pride Week parade went Saturday," said Captain Jones of the Council Bluffs Police Department. "It went beyond expectation. I am thrilled to see it go down this well. I'd say it's the biggest cooperative effort in recent Council Bluffs history." The effect of it all was well expressed in the words of a clinical psychologist, "It's got to be positive."[2]

Evelyn Hopper, a longtime Council Bluffs resident and a teacher with the Council Bluffs Schools who chaired the Pride Week Food Committee, said, "Saturday was one of the happiest days of my life. All those people in the park…it was absolutely amazing. But I didn't hear one complaint."[3] The people waited patiently in long lines to buy a hot dog for a quarter, a roast beef sandwich for half a buck, ice cream bars for fifteen cents, and a hot cup of coffee for ten cents.

Tammy McDowell, a junior in one of the Council Bluffs high schools, said, "You don't see things like this too often. It's easy to say Council Bluffs is boring. But with things like Pride Week, you really get a lot of people together for a good time."[4] Dave Tobias, a junior high teacher who served as the chairman for festivities at Bayliss Park, said, "It's been a lot of work, but it's been enjoyable." He summed up the spirit of Pride Week when he added, "We brought the community together. I think this is the beginning of a positive attitude in Council Bluffs. I think a lot of things will happen here now."[5] Mayor Walt Pyper said, "We've made a start on a new Council Bluffs, and there's no reason the renaissance shouldn't continue."[6]

To me, the purpose of Pride Week from the beginning was to instill enthusiasm in the community, to bring people together, and to create a sense of self-worth in the minds of young people. I believe people can do these things in cities all across the country. Young people look up to adults, and the type and quality of feelings we have about a place or a person are going to filter through to them. We must help them grow up with healthy self-concepts and an unshakable faith in God and the abilities He has given them to make a difference in their world.

My colleagues and I, of course, were delighted that the dream became a reality. The *Omaha World Herald* correctly portrayed my vision, "If Raj Chopra has his way, this spring's Council Bluffs Pride Week will be the biggest thing since the Hagenbeck Circus elephants visited Lake Manawa." Council Bluffs' *Nonpareil* proclaimed, "It was strictly big stuff. Big, big, big!"

Over thirty thousand people participated in one way or another. They came together, their spirits were high, and they were ready to launch a new beginning—a beginning of more positive respect for self and others. The wheels were set in motion. Every spring since 1979 the proud community of Council Bluffs has taken time to show its pride openly, and it renews itself to take on new challenges. It is a legacy passed on from year to year, with new leadership, new enthusiasm, new ideas, and new pride.

Early Results

I readily admit that I had certain misgivings and a deep-seated fear about accepting the Council Bluffs challenge. I knew that before we could boost the morale of staff and students, we had to boost the morale and image of the community. *And it could not wait three or five years.* It had to be done quickly before whatever momentum was there was lost and pessimism further deepened its roots. With the people's help and God's blessings it ended well. Hats off to the Council Bluffs people!

Our primary focus during the whole Pride Week endeavor was to improve public perception of Council Bluffs schools. The public was now willing to give us a chance to bring about educational improvements. But programs to foster public confidence can be sustained only if they are followed by reforms and student achievements. We went to work and developed detailed plans to tackle the key problems. Thinking good thoughts was not enough. We were forced to take some tough actions. And some of them hurt. I have listed some of them here.

1.   The number of *administrative staff was reduced* by twelve positions, and appropriate accountability was placed on the remaining administrators under a restruc-

tured organization. The organizational structure was changed from a role-based to a goal-based philosophy.

2. The *curriculum was reorganized* in sequential fashion with clear identification of concepts and objectives to be covered in one year. The teachers were given a voice in curriculum planning. Curriculum requirements for high school students were increased.

3. *Attendance requirements* were tightened, and strong follow-up measures were prescribed to deal with students who were absent without appropriate reasons. The juvenile court provided support and assistance.

4. *Promotional standards were set.* Social promotion—where students are moved to higher grades regardless of their ability or inability to meet academic objectives—was stopped. Students had to meet the criteria before they could be promoted.

5. A renewed *emphasis on test taking* was initiated. The test-taking climate was improved. Parental involvement in this program greatly benefited the students.

6. A *new code of conduct* was developed and strictly enforced to improve discipline. Violators were treated firmly. In-school suspension programs were implemented in high schools. Through counseling proper follow-up reduced the dropout rate.

7. With *better management of financial resources,* more money was channeled to new or expanded programs. A program for gifted students was broadened. Art education was introduced in the elementary schools.

The schools became more responsive to the community, and in turn, the citizens were again willing to identify with the schools. A sense of partnership developed. Within the schools themselves teacher morale and general attitude improved. Students' test scores reached a more respectable level.

The courage and vision of the board of education during this challenging time were beginning to pay dividends. People with foresight ran for the school board. In one case, a relative newcomer to the community—and a good leader—was elected, defeating a candidate who had been on the board for almost fifteen years. In fact, a new generation of community leaders enhanced the growth momentum by coming forward to run not only for seats on the school board but also for the city council and other elected bodies. The commitment and vision of the school board, supported by the positive attitude of the staff, were the catalyst that turned Council Bluffs around.

The people were not bad; the situations were bad. When CBS's "60 Minutes" blew into town and focused on the disharmony and disunity, it struck a dagger in the heart of the community. It is unfortunate that the people's successful efforts to turn this bad situation around did not receive equal publicity.

I found Council Bluffs people gentle, hard working, and giving. They wanted the best for their children. They did not want their school system to remain in turmoil. They were looking for the right person to help them make the situation good. I was fortunate to be chosen for that task.

From the generous, beautiful people of Council Bluffs I got what I was promised in the dream—"help." The turnaround came because the people wanted it so.

3

Finding My Purpose

Three years later, when Council Bluffs' civic and business leaders were polled on their opinion about the city's strengths and weaknesses, they ranked the school system as a community strength. An article in the *Omaha World Herald* (September 26, 1981) described interviews with three veteran Council Bluffs School Board members:

> Their school system has done an abrupt about-face since hitting a low point in 1976, when an uncomplimentary story was aired on CBS-TV's "60 minutes."...In separate interviews, all three referred to a recent meeting, "Council Bluffs 1999," at which community leaders split into 10 groups and listed the three most positive things about their city. All 10 included the schools.

John Moats, who served as president of the Council Bluffs School Board for two years during those challenging times, was quoted in the same article: "Four years ago, the schools would have been seen as among the most negative items."

What had changed?

Nothing, really—at least in terms of personnel. The

students, schools, teachers, and townspeople were essentially the same. Yet student test scores had soared to new highs, teacher morale was up, and parents were proud—so proud they had begun sponsoring the annual "Council Bluffs Pride Week" with a big parade down Main Street honoring their schools and community.

What made the difference?

Simply putting the principles of realistic thinking into action—"power principles," as I like to call them, had been put to work. I do not mean to imply that I alone brought these ideas to life. Countless people throughout the city caught the spirit as well, assisted by a sprinkling of new leaders in various elected positions who were ready and eager to shed the negative image and move ahead with new vitality and confidence.

And no matter where you are or what your obstacles, you can put these same attitudes to work, too. But like the oil deep in the earth, or the electricity in the air, these power principles will not do you any good unless you mine them, capture them, and apply them to specific situations. Like any new skill you learn, it takes practice, practice, practice.

A Faith Emerges

I did not become a realistic thinker overnight. My power principles surfaced after many years of setbacks and successes.

The year was 1947, and the India-Pakistan border had barely been established, dividing the two nations. Not political beliefs but religious ideologies had brought about the separation.

Our family lived in a village one hundred miles inside Pakistan. We were in great danger. Up to that time we had been one of the wealthiest families in our town. Our name was respected, and my early childhood was blessed with material abundance and a loving and caring family life. I was ten years old at the time this arbitrary religious boundary line left seven million Moslems in India and about six million Hindus inside Pakistan.

The Moslems were bent on making life miserable for the Hindus within their borders. The Indian government, trying to cope with problems of its newly acquired independence from Great Britain, was at first powerless to help. Multiplied thousands were killed in the ensuing religious riots. The personal price we as a family paid was the merciless murder of my mother's parents in another village about thirty-five miles from our home.

I remember distinctly the afternoon the bloodshed reached our own village. For several weeks, we had heard reports of rioting and massacres in other towns and villages. There were stories of homes' being burned, people murdered—but those were other villages, not our own. Now it was our turn.

For two and a half days, throngs of Moslems carrying knives, swords, and homemade weapons marched in our streets. I fled with my mother, two sisters, and a younger brother to the other side of town where we hid for eighteen hours in the basement of a friend's home. I can still hear the mob beating on the door, trying to enter the house to murder us hiding inside.

Only a few months before this nightmare took place, my father, at age thirty-two, had died suddenly of cancer. With a child's simple trust, I remember praying shortly before his death, "God, please make sure that my father stays with me." When a few days later I found my prayers were not answered the way I had asked, I was filled with anger and hatred. In my young mind, I doubted the very existence of God.

But in that dark, musty hide-out, enveloped by fear and uncertainty, I found myself praying feverishly again that this time God would listen. "God, protect us and help us get out of here alive," I pleaded.

On the morning of the third day of rioting, the streets fell silent, and we could hear the approach of the Indian army as it arrived to protect us and transport us across the border. As we emerged into daylight, we were shocked at the sight of the ravaged community we had always known as home. Bodies, strewn in the street, were being gathered to be cremated together in a common pyre. We heard stories of husbands who used their own swords to cut the throats of their wives and daughters in order to save them from humiliation and rape. I was sickened. The scene was one that would be burned permanently in my mind.

Overnight we had become refugees. Also overnight, an ever-so-slight flicker of faith and hope had been stirred in my heart. God—whoever He was—had protected me and my family. I knew it without question. My realization of His presence began at that moment. Like a sprouting acorn, my faith was but a seedling that needed both cultivation and care to realize its potential. It was as though a strong oak tree was just beginning to germinate. This seedling of faith in my heart would finally, in 1977, become an oak tree through a personal commitment to Jesus Christ and the nurture that comes from His teachings.

The Indian army transported us in trucks across the border to a refugee camp. As the oldest male in my family, I had to assume the role of provider. Our first thoughts were of survival. I started raising goats in the refugee camp so we could sell the milk to buy food and necessities for the family.

My paternal grandmother had stayed behind to protect our house and belongings, hoping we would eventually be able to return to our village. When that did not happen, she crossed the border and began the awesome task of looking for us in hundreds of refugee areas. A woman of great vision, she significantly affected my life as I matured to adulthood.

A Gift of Education

Grandmother found us after a search of nearly seven months. It was a day of celebration when we were reunited. She took one look at my shoeless feet and at the goats and said, "You have a greater purpose in life, Raj, than tending goats. You are somebody. You are going to get an education. God has a special plan for you."

By any educational standard, Grandmother was illiterate. She could not read or even write her name. And yet, providing for our education was of utmost importance to her.

Reluctantly I left my goat tending to return to school. But Grandmother's singleness of mind was a major stabilizing influence in my own life and in that of my family. She saw to it that we were sent off to school with breakfast in our stomachs, and she was there at the end of the day to discuss our studies. "Through education," she told us, "you will get abilities. Through abilities you will get confidence. And through confidence you will get the determination to search for your purpose in life. You must always dedicate yourself to making the best of the educational opportunities you have."

"Education," she would tell me later, "is a gift no one can steal from you. No fire can burn it, and no water can drown it. It will stand with you in good and bad times. Through education you can realize your dreams." Little wonder I ended up in the field of education.

You Are Somebody

When I graduated in 1958 from Punjab University in India with a liberal arts degree, I began the search for a job. In India at that time, it was very difficult for even college graduates to find employment. A new federal postal facility had just been opened in our city, and many of my friends applied for clerical positions there. I remembered my uncle, however, who had held a similar position and had never spoken with any pride about his work. Somehow I felt my purpose in life was to become something other than a clerk. My grandmother's message, "You are somebody; there is a purpose for your life," ran like a broken record through my mind.

I frequently traveled to New Delhi and stayed with an uncle there while I looked for work. A year and a half later, I still had no job, and I felt defeated. We had been living off our savings too long.

Finally, Mother arranged for me to have an interview with a gentleman who was an inspector of industries in a nearby town. He helped me secure a job as a salesman for a glass and plywood company in New Delhi. I was elated and went to work at 8:30 that first morning; I worked hard until 9:00 that night. The owner told me I had a bright future with his company because they were beginning to expand their business.

That evening as I left the store and walked to the bus stop, I thought about the way I had spent the day and then about Grandmother's words: *You are somebody.* I believe it was God who guided my feet to the railway station where I bought a postcard and addressed it to the owner and very deliberately wrote:

I thank you for giving me the job with your firm. After working one day, I know that my life has a purpose other than measuring glass and plywood for the rest of my life. There is something different in store for me.

Thank you.

Respectfully yours,

Raj Chopra

I mailed the postcard, but not without a twinge of remorse at giving up the job that I needed to help support my family. I was nevertheless filled with a strange sense of peace. When I wrote my mother of my actions, she was shocked, unable to understand what I had done. But my heart told me that God was beginning to work and move in my life. He had another plan for me.

The Attitude of Hope

I remember reading a story of Thomas Edison, the prolific American inventor, whose assistant complained to him one day: "Mr. Edison, we have tried five hundred experiments to find a solution to this problem. But we still haven't had any results." The inventor smiled and replied, "My friend, we do have results; we know five hundred ways that will not work."

It was another year and a half before I was offered another regular job. On that day, I had walked to the National Sports Stadium not far from my uncle's house. I met a former acquaintance who greeted me by asking, "Raj, how are things going? Have you found a job yet?"

I told him my story. He directed me to a man at the American School for diplomats' children in India. I went for an interview the next day. They were apparently impressed enough to agree to send me back to college to get my teaching certificate.

One year later, in 1962, I was teaching and coaching at the American School in New Delhi. It was a "dream" job. Never in my wildest imagination had I considered teaching, let alone working for the United States. I could not have been happier. At last I felt as though I was finding my unique purpose in life.

As I thought about a teaching career at the American School I recalled a childhood experience. I was in the eighth grade when a very special visitor spoke to our class. This man had just returned from his travels around the world, and he shared with us fascinating accounts of several countries.

At the end of his presentation, he talked for about ten minutes of his experiences in a country he described as "special," the "best," and "a land of milk and honey"— the United States of America. He talked eagerly about the auto industry and the tall buildings, and he especially mentioned the concept of freedom. He concluded with these words, "It is an exciting place to live, and anyone who is willing to work hard and who has the ability to dream can make the dream a reality."

This presentation left a firm and lasting impression on my mind. For days my fantasies would carry me to this fairyland of possibility. Through the avenue of my imagination I *did* visit the United States as I painted mental pictures of the beautiful land and its wonderful people.

As I grew older, my dreams of America faded, but nevertheless they had become a part of my subconscious mind at least, stored in my long-range memory bank.

Eleven years later, a new burning desire arose in me to pursue those earlier dreams. Going to the United States became an important goal, which I began to pursue with dedication and determination. This incident in the eighth grade and its later translation into a clearly defined objective, in fact, were the starting points for the goal-oriented concepts that have become such a strong part of my philosophy of life.

I worked hard and kept my sights on my goal to visit America. But I must admit that many times during the years 1962 to 1966 I seemed to make no progress toward my goal, and I was tempted to feel the whole idea was an impossible prospect.

Finally, the dream I had as an eighth grader became a reality fifteen years later. Early in 1966, I received the news that I was the recipient of a Ford Foundation Scholarship granted through the American School. It is difficult to describe the excitement, the sense of anticipation, and the real jubilation I felt over this great news.

Leaving family and friends behind, I set out on my great adventure. But after several months I felt selfish and alone.

I wanted my wife Sue to participate in and enjoy with me this beautiful American experience. In November 1966, she and our son Dick (whose second birthday was celebrated a month later) joined me. This family reunion was made possible with the assistance of officials in the College of Education at Bowling Green State University where I had enrolled.

After I completed my master's degree in July 1967, we returned to India. The U.S.A. had been my home for a year, and for Sue and Dick eight months. We had been richly blessed by the kindness and hospitality of many persons. We found the greatness of America not only in its beautiful fields, majestic mountains, foaming oceans, tall timberland, curling highways, skyhigh buildings, and advancement in science and technology but also in the giving, accepting, encouraging, and loving spirit of the American people.

Their beautiful spirit made us consider the possibility of moving permanently to the United States. I remembered many wonderful experiences we had during our brief stay (1966 to 1967). An experience with Mr. and Mrs. Ross, owner of the hotel where I spent the first night in Bowling Green, deserves mention.

On the second day in town I rented a small mobile home. That evening I discovered it had no bedding so I went downtown to purchase sheets, a blanket, and a pillow. To my amazement, all the shops closed by 6:30 P.M. I was also becoming aware that in Ohio beautiful, warm, sunny days changed to chilly evenings. Coming from the scorching June heat of India where there is but a few degrees drop in evening temperature, I was uncomfortably cold.

As I passed the Ross Hotel after my unsuccessful shopping expedition, I saw Mr. Ross standing by the main entrance. I greeted him, and he kindly invited me inside where we chatted in the hotel lobby. During our conversation, I mentioned my problem of the sheets and blankets. Mrs. Ross, who later joined in the conversation, heard from her husband about my difficulty. She quietly smiled, left the room, and soon returned with sheets, pillows, and blankets. She laid these in my arms and said, "You can return these whenever you have a chance to buy your own." I was overwhelmed by this act of kindness. I had been in the States for less than thirty-six hours, and the caring and sharing spirit had already begun to unfold. We made many friends and benefited tremendously from the kindness and friendliness of the American people.

During the first few months after our return to India in 1967, Sue and I found ourselves discussing the question: If we had a choice, where would we like to live? On the surface, it was a simple question, but the answer was far more complex. Our desire to move to the United States involved leaving parents, brothers and sisters, relatives, and friends. It involved leaving our properties and my secure, high-paying teaching position with the American School in New Delhi. It also meant taking new risks.

We spent the next sixteen months searching for an answer to the question we had jointly raised. After a great deal of contemplation and discussion, we made the decision to emigrate to America, the land of our choice. We felt proud of our Indian heritage and our country of birth. We were, however, physically, mentally, and spiritually to adopt another land as our country.

When I told my mother about our decision to emigrate, I explained to her our desire to pursue the American dream. It was difficult for her to understand why a person would leave a secure job, a bright future, family property, relatives, and friends to pursue something so obscure and uncertain. She also was genuinely concerned about the risk of going to another country with only a small amount of money and a suitcase full of clothes. In light of the realities she perceived, it seemed an unwise decision.

Sue and I had discussed all these eventualities, including possible failure. But the joy and exhilaration we felt over the thought of pursuing the American dream in a land of "we-can-and-we-will" provided us the positive momentum to move toward our goal. Finally we landed in New York in September 1969.

I enrolled again at Bowling Green State University in Bowling Green, Ohio, to begin work on my Ph.D. Already my goal was to become a superintendent of schools. With the help of many people, seven years later I captured the prize—my first superintendency was with the Bellefontaine City Schools in Ohio. Moving to Council Bluffs, Iowa, in 1978 and four years later assuming the superintendency of the nationally recognized Shawnee Mission School District in suburban

Kansas City were subsequent stages in that unfolding dream.

Keep Going

As an educator and administrator, I am often asked to speak before young peoples' groups, teachers, business and community leaders, and other similar organizations. Everywhere I go I attempt to point out some of the positive forces that have changed my life. "These principles can change your life too," I tell them.

Whether you are a business executive, housewife, teacher, or construction worker, you can be increasingly successful. You can make an impact on others' lives, overcome your fears and tension, and lead a more fulfilling life. But you must keep going when it seems easier to give up and stew in self-pity. A hopeful attitude increases your strengths and abilities and helps you to see a silver lining in any cloud of failure.

We do influence other lives daily, either positively or negatively. The choice is ours as to which it will be. Down deep, all of us hope to make a positive mark in this world, and the way to accomplish that is through right attitudes. Realistic thinking and living work to unleash boundless power with which we can literally move mountains.

Let us look at the principles that will help us handle the problems of life in a realistic and effective manner.

Part II

The Principles

4

Believe!

The old saying, "as a person thinks and believes, so shall he become," contains more truth than we might wish to admit. The power of believing, and its subsequent influence on our lives as a self-fulfilling prophecy, is well established through numerous research findings.

Belief lies at the very core of the power principles we will consider. Belief in the Lord, as well as belief in oneself because of Him and belief in others' capabilities and goals, constitutes the foundation upon which these principles are built. Without a strong commitment to God, to our own perseverance, and to others, we will find it difficult to see the good or expect the best. Successful living depends on one's commitment to believe. This philosophy can be summed up this way: *Believe* you can...

- look for the good
- be enthusiastic
- expect the best
- determine to make a difference

- love and laugh
- pursue the dream

The message I hear again and again when I speak to students and groups across the nation is that America is made up of people who believe in responsible freedom, for both themselves and the nation. In other words, we are a faith-oriented people. John Naisbitt, the author of *Megatrends,* notes that the United States is undergoing a revival in religious belief and church attendance. This, he says, is based on the fact that during turbulent times people desire structure, not ambiguity, in their lives. Similar reports are coming out of Eastern Europe, China, and Africa. The renewal of commitment, faith, and dedication is always a continuing process.

Structure provides us with rules for living. The power principles I have listed furnish guidelines that help make possible renewal, joyful living, and satisfying experience. We will consider these principles, one by one, in the remaining chapters of this book.

Daily Warm-up

I utilize a conditioning warm-up theory in my life. A runner, swimmer, baseball player, or any other athlete understands the importance of warming up before he or she hits the track or the playing field. But how many of us in business, academics, or other nonphysical endeavors prepare ourselves and approach our day with some kind of warming up for all the decisions, the stress, and the demanding mental activities that lie ahead?

I warm up daily with a simple count-your-blessings exercise. It is easy, and it takes only a few minutes. You can do it in front of the mirror while you are shaving or putting on your make-up. Begin by saying three good things about yourself. ("You're looking good today, [*your name*]. You certainly handled well that situation with your child [John] last night. You are learning to be a patient person—that's a real virtue in today's world!")

Next, list three good things about the place in which you live. ("I'm glad I live in the Kansas City area [or Minneapolis, or New York] because...") And last, name aloud three of your blessings. ("I'm blessed with a gentle and understanding husband [or wife]; a warm and cozy home; and a creative, inspiring career.")

Such a mental pep talk sets the tone for the day ahead. And that enthusiasm is carried one step further by daily affirming each family member's importance through hugs and a brief sharing time at the breakfast table. Discuss the expectations for the day ahead and verbally rehearse your blessings together. By accepting every day with a sense of gratefulness and thanksgiving, and by mentally warming up, our spirits are uplifted, and we are ready to expect the best in any situation.

Sometimes we are so bogged down with asking "Why me?" that we fail to see the beauty and charm of another day. Once while I was in an Omaha television station waiting to appear on a talk show, a cameraman who had visited my office many times for news stories walked by me. As we greeted each other, I commented that I had not seen him for some time. He told me that he had suffered a heart attack, and he had taken a long time to recuperate.

"Since that attack," he said, "I have developed an attitude of gratitude for every sunrise and every sunset. Before my illness, the birds chirping outside my window early in the morning always annoyed me. At times I'd even thought of getting my gun and shooting them. Now, hearing the sound of the birds is like a melody, and I tell myself that it's a beautiful day. I want to go out and do my best in a spirit of thankfulness. Life is a wonderful gift, and I want to celebrate it with joy and love."

If you are a student of the Bible, you will realize how well this outlook fits with what Paul said in the early chapters of the Book of Romans and in his other epistles about the importance of being thankful. King David of ancient Israel underscored the same importance of thankfulness in his psalms.

Dare to Dream

When I look back on some of my experiences, I realize what an impact faith in God and the resulting belief in myself and others have had in my moving forward in a positive fashion. Losing my father when I was only nine, becoming a refugee, and having to leave our home in Pakistan were anything but positive experiences for me and my family. Those were tremendous struggles for me and other young people to have to endure.

Our family literally went from riches to rags. Overnight I found myself standing in bread and blanket lines in the refugee camp. However, our deprivation at that time later became a positive force that was to impact our lives in all the years ahead.

Like Scarlett O'Hara in *Gone with the Wind*, realistic thinkers live by the philosophy that "tomorrow is another day." Unlike Scarlett, however, we do not bury our heads in the sand. We look to tomorrow with hope and expectation. Again and again we reiterate that "God has a purpose for me—He has a plan for me."

Because I am a native of India, my skin is a swarthy shade of brown. And although I have been in the United States since 1969, my English is still marked by a noticeable accent. When I was studying toward my doctorate in educational administration, I was strongly advised to pursue a career in higher education rather than in primary and secondary public schools. My advisors sensed that my Indian heritage and my accent might be a detriment to my career, but I persisted in trying to achieve my original goal. Perhaps my grandmother's repeated lessons on turning one's disadvantages into advantages upheld my determination in this matter.

Changing Disadvantages into Advantages

After I accepted the position as superintendent of schools in Bellefontaine, I quickly realized my national heritage was a real plus. It took only one photo in the local newspaper for my face to become quickly recognizable. In a very short time, the people knew who their new school superintendent was. "Oh, yes," they would say, "he's a native of India with an accent." I firmly believe that the recognition contributed to my rapid acceptance by the community. Seeing my picture in the newspaper and hearing my voice on radio or television, citizens quickly developed a special association with their new superintendent.

I remember an incident where my foreign appearance played an important role in making a bad situation good. In 1979, at the height of the American hostage crisis in Iran, I was in Bismarck, North Dakota, on a speaking engagement. At the airport afterward, I did not hear the boarding announcement for my flight back to Omaha. Planes had been taking off, and only two remained on the ground.

I noticed that on one of these, the door was about to be closed, ready for takeoff. I happened to ask another traveler, "Do you know where that plane is going?"

He replied, "Omaha."

I dashed out the door and ran toward the plane, wildly waving my briefcase. (You must know that missing a plane in Bismarck may very well translate into spending another twelve to twenty-four hours there!)

A ground crew member saw me running toward the plane and followed me in hot pursuit. As he came closer I heard language that ought not be repeated. It suddenly dawned on me that from my appearance I may very well be perceived as an Iranian. He no doubt was fearful I might be trying to hijack or blow up the plane. Noticing his intent to tackle me, I quickly threw my briefcase on the ground and raised my arms in a sign of surrender. "No English!" I shouted, smiling broadly as I did so.

The attendant burst into laughter and signaled the pilot to open the door and lower the steps. I climbed aboard and settled into my seat with a thankful sigh. I did not open my mouth until I reached Omaha!

When I talk about believing as being realistic in our thinking, I do not mean using blind faith to give ourselves a psychological con job. Instead I mean perceiving seemingly impossible tasks with an attitude of realistic faith.

Some people in India used to catch elephants and train them for heavy work tasks. The animals were taught to move great logs from one place to another and load them on ox carts to be hauled to nearby sawmills. The elephants were also important to these people for personal convenience and commercial transportation.

The challenging task was not only to catch the elephants but also to train them in as short a time as possible so that valuable production time in the lumber operations would not be lost. Over the years, the villagers developed a very creative way of quickly training the animals to obey the commands of their masters.

After first spotting a wild elephant, the villagers

would circle the beast. With their drums, pots and pans, and other noise-making equipment they would gradually direct the animal toward a prepared trap—a carefully camouflaged pit into which the elephant would fall. As a team, the villagers would work swiftly to secure the elephant with ropes and chains and then pull the mighty beast out of the hole.

Next, they would tie its front legs to a banyan tree—a tree with a huge trunk. The elephant would immediately begin its effort to break the chain or the tree. This struggle could continue for days, depending on the animal's ability to withstand the stress and strain of trying to free itself. Food was withheld from the elephant during this time in order to weaken its resolve and hasten its submission.

At last, the elephant's master and trainer would notice that the hungry beast had accepted its helplessness and quit its struggle. The villagers would gather to pat the animal and give it a little food. They would continue to keep the elephant tied to the tree, however, and reward it with food and water for accepting its captivity.

After a number of days, when the elephant had completely given up its struggle, the villagers would place a small peg in the ground and with a small rope would tie one of the elephant's front legs to the peg. What they now had was the strongest animal of the forest tied with a weak rope to a mere peg in the ground. Why didn't the elephant break the rope and escape? Simply because he had been made to believe he could not do it. Thus he never tried.

If we believe we are unable to do a task, even our abilities and strengths will fail us. Conversely, believing we can make a bad situation good taps unrealized resources of strength. We have all heard stories of mothers and fathers who suddenly gained unknown strength when a heavy object has fallen on their child. When they later return to the scene, they find they are totally unable to lift that same item. Where did that superhuman strength come from? "You can if you think you can" goes the old adage.

A believing person is like the spaceship that must draw on tremendous reserve power to rise from the launching pad and reach its orbital speed. We have at our disposal a power resource to counter the forces that would hold us down. That reserve is found in belief or faith.

Being Determined

While I was serving as an assistant superintendent with the Medina (Ohio) City School District, I met a very successful businessman who had a severe case of stuttering. One day he shared with me that during his school days he was advised by his teachers and counselors that he had no future in any job requiring contact with the public. The inference, as he saw it, was that he should be shoved into some place like the boiler room. Unfortunately, the attitude of his parents was no different from that of his teachers.

But he took as a challenge the suggestion that he avoid public contact. He was determined to prove all of them wrong. He worked hard and continued to develop high expectations of himself and an unshaken determination to become "somebody."

Today this gentleman is a highly successful businessman with the direct responsibility of dealing with government officials and corporate executives. With great courage and belief in himself, he refused to accept the narrow limits that others were trying to place on him.

Recently, I visited with a teacher who had for some

time been trying to obtain an administrative position but without success. As she shared her frustrations, I told her she was giving me three nonverbal messages: First, that she did not believe in herself. Second, that she had lost her enthusiastic approach to life's challenges. And third, that her general attitude appeared to be negative.

I suggested she explore her options with a firm belief that by becoming an administrator, she would be able to help a larger number of students. Students and their well-being must be the prime focus of her thoughts, I told her. Also, she must believe in her own capabilities and purpose in life and free herself of the negative idea that she had not been treated fairly in the past. Look for your strengths, I emphasized, warm up your spirit, and *believe*.

About a month later, I heard the good news that she had been appointed principal of a school in a neighboring district. I happened to meet her a few days after she had the job offer, and she said, "Oh, yes, I was feeling down the day I talked with you. I was frustrated and unsure. But your reminder really helped me realize that though positive thinkers might not succeed all the time they do know how to handle failure and frustration better than negative thinkers. It gave me another perspective—a more positive one." She wrote me later, "You have had such a tremendous influence on my life and were so instrumental in helping me with the identification of positive action as well as positive thinking."

By believing we *can* change our failures to successes. But sometimes we have to stand the test of failure and try again and again. With a positive attitude and a belief in our purpose, we stand a better chance of success.

Inspiration from Students

As an administrator, I always enjoy visiting students and teachers in their classrooms. These visits are inspiring because of the honesty and candor of students' responses and of their interaction with me. I also delight in watching the master teachers at work, not only instructing in reading, writing, or mathematical skills but also encouraging and praising the students, touching their aspirational levels. These outstanding teachers are continuously searching for opportunities to strengthen the confidence levels of their students and promoting the "you can" attitude through their own positive attitudes.

During one of these visits in May 1983, I talked with a group of fifth-grade students. The school principal had asked me to share with this class some of my observations about success.

I decided to try to involve the students by exploring the topic through dialogue. I hoped to arouse their thinking and reasoning processes. Though my goal was clear to me, I wanted to be sure the students felt an ownership of the ideas brought out in our discussion. I wanted them to consider our "success steps" as their own, not just mine.

As the discussion progressed, we developed the following steps to success:

1. Believe in yourself.
2. Develop a "can do" attitude.
3. Try again and again, and never quit.
4. Work hard.
5. Help others.

We discussed each step, and students shared the special meaning of these principles from their own perspectives. They were assured at the outset that their perception of each idea was as significant and important as anyone else's. This helped even the shy and withdrawn students to participate and articulate their feelings.

The students were realizing growth in the affective domain as well as learning the meaning of self-worth. They were recognizing that all of us do not succeed every time. I told them that being of service to others without expecting financial rewards was, in my opinion, of highest importance to every student's success in education and in later adult life. Together we were exercising our abilities to think realistically, to communicate our thoughts to the rest of the class in a logical fashion, and to develop speaking skills in front of a group.

In the course of our conversation about success, I asked the students what "believing in yourself" meant to them personally. As might be expected, different students communicated different meanings. I was somewhat puzzled, though, when one student said, "Believing means to me freedom." I nodded and went on to the next student.

As I drove back to my office, the student's answer remained in my thoughts. I had not further questioned the student so as not to place him on the spot. Perhaps, I suspected, his answer may not have been well thought out.

Then the thought suddenly struck me—what a brilliant answer! I had failed to adequately praise the student for his answer, but more importantly I did not allow the other students to absorb the deeper meaning of freedom he had expressed. I was looking at freedom from a political perspective only while he meant freedom from our self-imposed limitations!

How many struggles are we willing to undertake to maintain our political freedom? Historically, our forebears have been willing to make the highest possible sacrifices. The call for American independence in 1776 and my own personal experience of the struggle for independence in India point out the awesome price people are willing to pay for freedom.

But the struggle to free ourselves from self-imposed limitations is as vital to realizing our inner potential as any battle for political freedom. This young fifth-grade student had unearthed for me a whole new meaning for believing and freedom. We must work to free ourselves from these limits by recognizing the incredible natural drive of the human mind and body.

All of us have within us unharnessed powers. People who do not believe will always live in the captivity of self-placed limits.

The Mind's Power

By unleashing the power of our minds and believing in ourselves, we can focus on our strengths and become whatever we want to become. Dr. Norman Vincent Peale discusses in one of his books a personal experience that occurred soon after he graduated from college. As a young minister, he was serving as the American Legion's chaplain in Kings County, New York.

It was soon after World War I. He had been invited to give the invocation at a Memorial Day meeting in Brooklyn's Prospect Park. Shortly before the ceremony, he found his name listed on the printed program as the main speaker. Peale writes, "I gulped. Indeed, I froze. I had no speech prepared."

He immediately confronted the master of ceremonies about the mistake on the program. Colonel Theodore Roosevelt, Jr., son of President Theodore Roosevelt, was present that afternoon. He overheard the conversation and intervened, "What's the matter, son? Are you afraid?"

Peale frankly admitted to being more than afraid.

Roosevelt suggested that he think of the "Gold Star

Mothers" in the audience. "Each one of them has lost a son in the war," Roosevelt said. "Why don't you think of them, rather than thinking of yourself?" He encouraged young Peale to "think courage" and go ahead and give the speech. Peale did.[1]

All of us are confronted with situations in life where we fail to believe creatively that there is an answer to our dilemmas! We are overcome by our lack of self-confidence.

People whom we admire and respect today are generally those who have faced such situations and have used them as positive experiences to build on. We need to look at each situation as a new possibility and another opportunity.

In a recent speech, Dr. Jonas Salk, the discoverer of the polio vaccine, emphasized the power of the mind and challenged his listeners to work to overcome what he calls the "crippling of the mind." We must remove the limits from our thinking.

Marva Collins, who left her public school teaching position and opened West Preparatory School in Chicago, believes that every student has the ability to learn. She *expected* her students to learn and, in turn, they responded to her faith in them. The result was a high level of learning and achievement. Marva Collins has the ability to touch and raise the aspirational level of her students. Other teachers can do the same thing if this becomes important to them—and I know that for many of them it *is* important.

Fight the Odds—and Persist!

After having spent two and a half rewarding years as assistant superintendent with the Medina, Ohio, school system, I felt a rekindling of my earlier yearning to be a superintendent. In January 1976, I sent applications all over the United States for any and all possible superintendent openings. By June 1 I had applied to over two hundred school districts.

At the time I was mailing my applications, I did not realize the personal price I would have to pay as the replies came back. Beginning in February 1976, I received letters, sometimes two or three at a time, stating, "Your qualifications are excellent, but you are not suited for our district."

For a few weeks I was able to keep an upbeat, positive attitude and expect the best the next day. Soon, however, the rejection mail became unbearable. I needed "mental ventilation" in order to keep a positive perspective in this challenging but discouraging situation. As I mentioned earlier, the advice I had received from some of my college professors was to pursue higher education administration, not public school administration. Was this advice correct after all? I was starting to believe that my foreign nationality must be the detriment. As doors kept closing, this adversity was beginning to affect my inner being.

I am blessed to have a wife whose spirit of realistic optimism is seldom diminished. One day, in despair, we looked each other in the eyes and said almost in unison, "Our lives have a purpose. God is going to help us." We discussed the highlights of our experiences and how far we had come with God's help.

This realization restored our faith, and the letters of rejection no longer discouraged us. We strongly believed that the right opportunity would come, and we decided not to permit ourselves to be engulfed with bitterness from the rejections. For bitterness is like an acid that burns us from the inside and only serves to perpetuate a defeatist attitude.

Life Begins Whenever You Want It To

We all need to exercise faith in one particular area—life's later years, mistakenly and unfortunately referred to as the declining years. Whether you are young or old or in-between, do not stop believing in yourself just because of age. History is full of stories of men and women who have refused to view their retirement as the end of life. For them retirement has been a new beginning, not an end. These people have looked forward to the adventure of retirement with a firm faith and a sense of anticipation. They have caught their second wind as they embraced another important phase of life and service to humanity.

Dr. James F. Fries, a gerontologist with Stanford University Medical Center, wrote in the *New England Journal of Medicine* that the biological limitations of an individual are closely related to his or her attitude toward life. Dr. Fries is of the opinion that "the body, to an increasing degree, is now felt to rust out rather than to wear out."[2]

Dr. Fries's conclusion is borne out by many historical and present-day personalities who have commonalities in believing their lives are of continuing purpose and service. They strongly believe that life is a limitless gift and should be spent in service to others. Therein lies the secret of continuing self-fulfillment. Look at these examples:

- Pablo Casals (1876–1973) had a strong desire to live in spite of his infirmities and performed as a cellist and conductor well into his nineties.
- Adolph Zukor (1873–1976) at ninety-one was chairman of Paramount Pictures.
- Anna Mary Robertson Moses (1860–1961) took up

painting as a hobby at age seventy-six. Better known as "Grandma Moses," she won international fame and staged fifteen one-woman shows throughout Europe.

- Pablo Picasso (1881–1973) completed his portraits of "Sylvette" at seventy-three, married for the second time at eighty, then executed three more series of drawings between eighty-five and ninety.
- Golda Meir (1898–1978) became prime minister of Israel at seventy-one and held the post for five years.
- Pope John XXIII (1881–1963) became pope at seventy-seven.
- Konrad Adenauer (1876–1967) at age seventy-three became the first chancellor of the Federal Republic of Germany and held the position for fourteen years.
- Artur Rubinstein (1887–1982) gave one of his greatest piano concerts at New York's Carnegie Hall at age eighty-nine.
- Dr. Albert Schweitzer (1875–1965), Nobel laureate for peace, lived to the age of ninety serving the needy in Africa.
- Bob Hope celebrated his eighty-first birthday in 1984, and he still brings humor and laughter into our lives through his television appearances. He continues his performances for men and women in the armed services.
- Mother Teresa, though seventy-four at this writing, faithfully serves the poorest of the poor. A 1979 recipient of the Nobel Peace Prize, she follows a rigorous daily schedule of service and sacrifice to humanity. Her message of love is a ray of hope for thousands of destitute people in Calcutta, India.
- Ronald Reagan became the oldest president of the

United States when at sixty-nine he took the oath of office in January 1981.

- Dr. Norman Vincent Peale, author of over forty books on successful living through positive thinking and a great American orator, is still actively serving mankind at age eighty-five.

All these men and women have believed their lives have a continuing purpose and consider service to others as an important focus of their lives. Their desire to help others and make a contribution to humanity has undoubtedly contributed to their longevity.

In contrast, famous violinist Niccolo Paganini willed his violin to the city of his birth, Geno, Italy, with the condition that the violin never again be played. Yet the absence of use and handling results in the decay of the wood used in the instrument. It is ironic that Paganini's wish has resulted in the crumbling of the precious violin in its case.

Each of us needs to look for and believe in his or her unique purpose. The starting point is found in that simple word: *believe.* But do more than just start. Learn to continue believing, despite obstacles and setbacks.

5

Look for the Good

You have a unique and special purpose in this world. Yes, you! Perhaps you have already discovered it, and you are flying high on the wings of success and self-fulfillment. Or maybe you are in that unfolding stage where your special mission in life is not yet clear.

I hope, though, if you are in this latter category, you are actively in pursuit of that purpose. Herbert Otto says, "Change and growth take place when a person has risked himself and dares to become involved with experimenting with his own life." That is also called "sticking your neck out," or being a risk-taker. To do that, you must believe that when you are called to a task, you can pull it off. You let go of all those crippling fears and go for it! People who are willing to take risks free themselves from fear, and they take these risks knowing they may meet with failure.

But there's something else here. Believing *I can* also means believing *you can*.

Believing you can is a freeing experience. Believing others can is even better.

As an educator, I feel very strongly that school personnel have a powerful impact on the self-concept of our nation's young people. In fact, this may be the most important factor in their whole educational experience.

Children who realistically believe in themselves and their ability to accomplish great things will discover early in life their own unique inner powers. We have a responsibility as educators and parents to see to the well-being of our children, to help them develop positive self-concepts, and to inspire them to reach their full potential.

As I noted in the last chapter, Marva Collins saw a special purpose in her life. She cashed in her teacher's pension in order to start her school. She saw wonderful qualities in her students and made the potential drop-outs successful. She said, "I looked those children in the eye and told them, 'I will not let you fail. You are the brightest children in the whole world. And I want each of you to know that the words "I can't" are a lie.' "[1]

Accentuate the Positive

To make progress in any situation, you have to start with what is right about it and build on that. You must be able to see the good in a bad situation.

I am reminded of Red Schoendienst, famed second baseman of the St. Louis Cardinals in the 1940s and 1950s. He was chosen many times for the All-Star game and held numerous fielding records. Once, in the fifth inning of a game with Milwaukee, Red was hit in the right eye by a ball glancing off his bat. The eye immediately puffed up. As he was being removed from the field on a stretcher, instead of indulging in self-pity, Red said he was thankful it hit his right eye. If it hadn't, "I wouldn't be able to see the pitcher very well."

You can learn to overcome the odds by seeing the

good in each situation you face. Dr. Edith E. Eger, executive director of the El Paso Center for Marital and Family Therapy, recently spoke to the Shawnee Mission School District. She and her sister were prisoners in a concentration camp during the Holocaust. "Our captors took us to a room where, along with other women, we were asked to strip down. Our bodies and heads were shaved to humiliate and degrade us," she told us. "My sister had beautiful long hair, which she always nurtured with care and tenderness. After our heads were shaved, my sister asked me, 'How do I look?' Of course, she looked funny without her beautiful long hair. But I looked at my sister, and with all the love in my heart that I could muster I replied, 'You have beautiful eyes!' "

That is the way to look, feel, and think in a bad situation. Try to make it good. But for most of us, it does not happen overnight. Creative, realistic thinking takes practice.

When I accepted my first principalship in 1970, I walked into a school that had developed a long history of disciplinary problems. A newspaper reporter aroused the anger of the proud area residents when he described the school as "the trouble spot" in the school district.

Because of the discipline problems, I began standing in the doorway every morning to greet the children as they came in to school. As each child walked through the door, I would say something like, "Good morning, I'm glad you're here!" During that ten- to fifteen-minute period I would greet some three hundred students.

Gradually, I began to know many of them on a personal basis. I would call them by name, compliment them on a school project they had completed successfully, or ask about their family. The excitement generated by that simple act was thrilling.

I mixed very firm discipline with strong doses of love. They clearly understood my expectations of their behavior. I was no pushover, believe me. But I was committed to mixing the tough with the tender. The students' response to this new treatment was dramatic. Every morning I openly accentuated the good in these children.

One morning as I was greeting students, one of them placed a dollar bill in my hand. When I looked at him with a puzzled expression, he blurted out, "I'm sorry. Last night I was not careful, and I broke the school window with a baseball." What a transformation in this young boy's attitude!

In another instance, in order to prove my firmness and to get the attention of a perpetually troublesome boy and his parents, I had to take him to juvenile court. It was an extreme move, but this boy came around to good behavior—and it happened only through this dramatic process. We may see the potential for good in others, but sometimes firm action is needed to bring it out. I know of many principals and teachers who are successfully motivating their students by using both warmth and warning to create a more positive, realistic learning climate.

Confronting the Bad

As I work with students, I remind them of their responsibilities to fellow students, to friends, and to members of the community. I tell them they are good people and that I trust them. It is thrilling to see the disciplinary problems begin to diminish. As children realize that someone cares about them and that they are respected in their school setting, they behave in a more responsible manner. We must remember that students at times try our patience just to test our caring attitude for them.

I remember a particular incident that occurred while I was principal of an elementary school. I had been carrying my message of trust, respect, responsibility, and love to the students. I always attempted to help them understand my expectations as well as the consequences of any wrong actions.

One afternoon some girls clogged the wash basin in the restroom by stuffing paper towels into the drain. As a result, the restroom was flooded. When it was brought to my attention, I was told who might have been responsible—a sixth-grade student I will call Brenda. I called her to my office.

"Brenda, I have been told that you might be responsible for placing the paper towels in the drain, which has caused flooding in the girls' restroom." Brenda looked surprised and denied the accusation.

So I continued, "Brenda, if you say you didn't do it, then I will believe you for I know you are a responsible person. I respect you for being responsible and I trust you." I sent her back to the classroom.

Later that day, her teacher came to my office and said, "What did you say to Brenda? She came back from your office and began to cry."

I called Brenda back to my office. I asked her what had happened to make her cry.

"I am the one who caused the flooding," she confessed. "I was upset because of what you said about trusting me and my being a responsible person. I felt bad that I hadn't lived up to your trust."

I put my arm around her and told her I was proud of her for confessing her wrongdoing, explaining that we all make wrong decisions and that it takes real courage to admit it. We both learned an important lesson that day.

Accentuating the positive in our lives and in others is not overlooking our errors. It is, instead, facing our shortcomings and dealing head-on with them. And it is not always easy.

A teacher at one of my schools seemed to have an excessively gloomy attitude. In the teachers' lounge she would criticize everything from the administration to the school lunches to the weather outside. Several of the other teachers had complained to me of her attitude. After a while, her negativism rubbed off on teachers around her.

Toward the end of the year I met with her and discussed the problem. We talked about reaching out to others, instead of always complaining, and offering help, when appropriate, to correct problems. She agreed to try.

At the beginning of the next school year this teacher was quite obviously trying very hard to be cheerful, almost overeager to help others on the teaching staff. The first impression of many of her colleagues was that she was only pretending. Her new role as a team member and self-appointed cheerleader was considered by some a sham. But by the end of that year, her cheery countenance was decidedly natural.

Her peers, who at the beginning felt the change in her attitude was a camouflage over her generally pessimistic attitude, were forced to accept the change as genuine. As she continued her supportive attitude, the feedback reinforced her behavior. One would never have guessed that this lady had once carried a black cloud with her wherever she went. She became addicted to being positive and helpful to others.

Doing good is habit forming. The intrinsic rewards for making bad situations good are too many for a person to follow a course of self-imposed despair. Seeing the positive side takes hard work and practice, but eventually it can become second nature in one's approach to living.

The Good Is Sometimes Hard to Find!

Once a friend who was about to be interviewed for a principal's position called me for advice. She was distressed that a couple of individuals in her particular school felt her unqualified for the position and were campaigning hard against her appointment. She was, of course, discouraged.

I suggested to her that focusing on those persons who were hurting her only fostered hateful thoughts that shut off her creative thoughts. "Think about those people who have helped you along in your career," I encouraged her. "Thoughts of those people will serve you to uplift you. You will be imaging the remembrance of helping people rather than the ugliness of hurting people."

I elaborated on my philosophy of personal relationships. "Try to love the unlovables. You can control your attitude and thus maintain a positive and hopeful climate. Believe in your purpose and apply yourself to the pursuit of the job. Overcome fear of the interview by visualizing the people you can help if you are selected."

Later I was delighted by not surprised to receive a call from her that she had been chosen for the job.

One of the best stories illustrating what I mean by seeing the good appeared in the Council Bluffs *Nonpareil* a few years ago. The reporter had done an excellent profile on a couple in their eighties who had just been married. At the end of the interview the reporter wrote, "I asked the newlywed couple what was the best part of their lives. They both stared at me. Then the woman spoke out with confidence and firmness, 'That has yet to come.'"

What a beautiful way to look at life! This couple was looking fondly ahead to their years together with a sense of realistic anticipation. Life was not all over for them.

They believed in drinking the elixir of life to the last drop.

What Council Bluffs Taught Me

I have already related some of the deep reservations I had about accepting the superintendent's post in Council Bluffs. During the time I was deliberating on this decision, I was offered a similar position in an affluent, well-established school district in Wisconsin. From the outset, the Wisconsin job looked like a much easier, more comfortable situation. As in Robert Frost's delightful poem, "The Road Not Taken," my choice of the path made the difference.

On the untraveled road there are obstacles. But to conquer one's fear of them and to take the necessary risks make choosing this road beautiful and rewarding. Part of the joy comes in clearing the trail for others to enjoy. Through your efforts, others will find a new freedom—freedom from fear and limitations. Your reward will come in being the pathfinder who helps make our society a better place in which to live, to grow, and to share.

I was so smothered by the negativism I encountered during that fateful indoctrination trip to Council Bluffs, I failed to look for the many dedicated and good citizens there who would be my support. The very first week I was in my new office, I had an unexpected visit from two dynamic, enthusiastic teachers who had just returned from an educational conference in St. Louis. Their excitement bubbled over as they shared some of the ideas they had gleaned from the meetings—things they felt could help the students in Council Bluffs.

It was as if a light bulb went on for me. I realized that in order to see the good in this community, I was going to have to go out and *look* for the good. An enemy had hid it from me. Willing and dedicated people are in every community or organization. In any tough situation, the best hope is to start working with them from the realistic side.

Let me suggest you take an inventory to the plus side of the greatest problem you currently are facing. Use my model if you wish. Here is how I began to analyze the strengths and weaknesses of the school system at Council Bluffs. The balance sheet came out something like this:

What Caused the Negatives?

1. The Council Bluffs School District was about to undergo a full-scale investigation by the federal Department of Health, Education, and Welfare concerning complaints of discrimination in the educating of children and the hiring of teachers.

2. Two years before, a testing program showed that Council Bluffs' high school students ranked lower in achievement compared with both Iowa and national averages. This produced an outcry from parents concerning the quality of the district's education program.

3. Friction among school board members, parents, administration, and teachers frequently brought disruption during board meetings, causing some educators to look elsewhere for jobs. A board member described the system as "sick" and another board member referred to board meetings as the "best show in town."

4. When the board first voted on my application, the margin to hire me was 5-2. It was later changed to 6-1, but was still not unanimous. Their support was important to me and would have to be earned.

What Were the Opportunities?

1. The board had taken a new turn, and the majority were decidedly interested in bringing quality education to the district. New board members brought a new sense of optimism, a sharper focus, and a desire to restore good education.

2. There were many good people in the community ready to support any positive initiatives in the school district.

3. There were many more dedicated teachers in the system than the community realized.

4. The students were like students anywhere—fully capable of rising to impressive levels in both test scores and overall performance if properly motivated and guided.

5. The business community had expressed a desire to play an active role in helping the schools regain momentum.

6. Local pastors and churches were sincerely interested in supporting the schools.

7. District administrators were well qualified and eager to turn around the system's image.

8. The system, thanks to the Iowa State School Finance Law, was in stable financial condition.

9. A new junior high school was under construction.

10. The community was ready to rally around a new superintendent.

It was clear to me that there were many positives here on which to build. With this new perspective of realism, my basic elements of enthusiasm and optimism returned. I, too, was ready to rally around the school system, its dedicated teachers, administrators, and the good people in the community who sincerely wanted to see the good in their school system.

Do you see the realistic approach to the challenge here? When I talk of a positive approach toward making a bad situation good, I do not mean thinking your way around the problems as though they do not exist. Rather, I mean assessing the difficulties, believing they can be solved, and then moving to conquer the problems by finding out what is good in the situation and working on the strength of those positive elements.

What appeared at first to be an impossible mission in Council Bluffs was simply a lesson in proper attitude. It meant looking at our problems as opportunities and *accentuating the positive.* I found Council Bluffs people proud and eager to help.

I also learned the important lesson there that the quality of education in the schools has an important relationship to the quality of the school board. This body, by serving as a good role model, provided positive momentum toward conflict resolution and growth. A board of education that continuously looks for faults without recognizing achievement is a liability. A mixture of critical analysis and praise makes possible due recognition of persons who have earned commendation. Accentuating the positive makes all the difference.

What about "Bad Press"?

Let us examine the problem of handling the news media. Local newspapers and TV and radio stations can often break a business, a politician, a church, or a school system by reporting only the defects they see. That is news! And it *sells.* Because of that, some school board members and superintendents get hypersensitive and assume that the media are only out to do a hatchet job. (And sometimes there is ample reason for concern!)

When I got to Council Bluffs, it was only natural that in the wake of the exposé by the "60 Minutes" program, a lot of people were sensitive about the media. But I decided to look instead at the plus side. I started by accepting the obvious fact: reporters do not work as our public relations agents. Their purpose is (1) to sell their services profitably and (2) to inform the public of community affairs—in that order. So we set out to be completely open with them and try to help them succeed in both areas.

We also realized it was our job as educators to feed them good news. They had no problem finding the bad! Each day of the week we tried to give the media at least one good story about the school system. And that was not difficult to do. A school can have as many inspiring human interest stories as it has pupils. But you have to look for them. When we found such stories, we passed them along.

Of course, even with our "good news" efforts, the media at times carried something that we did not like. When they did a number on us, all we did was smile and say, "Well, we really took it on the chin that time. But one of these days we'll get a good story from you!" We learned to work with, not against, reporters, looking upon them as basically decent people, which they are.

Again, people usually respond to your expectations. If you believe they are good, one way or another, consciously or unconsciously, they are going to respond with goodness. I expected the media to be fair. Occasionally I reminded them of the awesome responsibility of public trust they carry. They will have public confidence as long as they are willing to stand the same scrutiny as they place on other institutions. The worst thing that once happened was when a reporter came to me with preconceived conclusions that were incorrect. Although the interview demonstrated his ideas were wrong, his story came out with his original misconceptions.

The following strategy of working with the media has

served me well over the years:

1. Be open and communicative. Use simple, clear language so that the reporter cannot misinterpret what you say.

2. Avoid professional jargon and the "no comment" syndrome.

3. If you call the news media to cover the good news, also be available to respond to unfavorable news. We lose credibility by not being available and responsive.

4. Let the reporters know you as a person. Know your reporters as persons. Do not expect any favors.

5. If something is written that you do not like, do not call the reporter to criticize or berate. If facts are incorrectly reported, draw the reporter's attention to the error in a positive fashion without placing the reporter in a defensive posture. Remember, reporters are human and have egos. They want to be on the front page, and it is usually easier to accomplish this by a sensational or controversial story.

6. If you like a particular story, make sure to compliment the reporter without patronizing or flattering.

7. Make sure that your reporters have your home phone number so they can call you in special situations.

8. Visit the newspaper office whenever you can.

9. Be willing to speak on issues directly rather than through intermediaries.

10. Be optimistic and hopeful.

Look for the good; do good; spread good. You will feel good. They are all interconnected. And there should always be a degree of urgency in your search for the good side of things. How so? Because life is like a bubble of water.

When the Bubble Bursts

Make sure you do your best today because tomorrow the bubble may burst. This concept was brought home to me one fall evening as I joined a group from school to watch a demonstration of endurance, strength, and enthusiasm by students participating in the Shawnee Mission invitational cross-country competition.

Suddenly, with no warning, an experienced and dedicated runner, Ryan Young, staggered and collapsed in the midst of the meet. A doctor present on the scene and the paramedics tried to revive him. I witnessed the fear and uncertainty on the faces of the medical professionals as they did everything in their power to bring back Ryan. A few hours later in a local hospital, Ryan Young died at the age of sixteen.

Ryan loved running. He overcame earlier handicaps to compete, and his goal was to win a school athletic letter. (He won that letter before he died.) Principal Dean Johnson read the following statement to the Shawnee Mission West High School student body on October 17, 1983, where Ryan had been a junior.

Today will be Ryan Young Day at Shawnee Mission West. As most of you know, Ryan's funeral will be held today. His last living act was to run in the cross-country race Friday at Shawnee Mission Park.

As you begin another week of school today think of your attitude. It is easy to take each day for granted. Perhaps to even become bored with the routine of our lives. We sometimes forget how important any given day may be.

All that anyone can do is to *try very hard* in our individual work and assignment. Ryan did that. He ran and ran; many hours, and many miles. He did his best. We can learn from him and begin on this day to live our lives to the fullest and give our best each day since we do not know which day it is in our life.

Do not put off utilizing the good in your life another day. Start now to practice and condition yourself to see the good.

Do you like that dress your wife is wearing? Say so! Did your subordinate just complete a report and hand it over to you a day early? Let him or her know you appreciate it! Indeed, praise is one of the important elements of this particular power principle. Seeing the good must be followed by articulation.

Seeking Good Does Not Mean Denying the Bad

Have you by now painted a mental Pollyanna image of this jolly school superintendent who glad-hands his way around the community and cheerfully extols only the goodness of his infallible school system? Wrong! Accentuating the positive does not mean ignoring poor production or settling for mediocre performance.

In any organization, whether public or private, people make the difference. A spirit of cooperation and trust helps everyone to pull together toward common goals. The involvement of people within the organization in the goal-setting process gives them a sense of pride and ownership of the goals. As managers, we must assure ourselves that those goals are achievable and that the goals fit not only the abilities of the person involved but also his or her special interests.

In leading people to see the good in others or in the organization itself, here is a list of helpful do's:

1. Outline your expectations in clear and precisely defined terms, and in cooperation with the employee,

transform those expectations into goals. Doing this will help develop mutual understanding.

2. After goals have been established, the supervisor should offer the employee flexibility and support in accomplishing them.

3. Clearly communicate the desired results and the criteria for measuring those results.

4. Offer praise for progress toward the accomplishment of goals.

5. The slipshod job should result in immediate confrontation. In doing so, draw attention first to the person's strengths and virtues. Like my story of young Brenda, we must convey to those we are managing or teaching that they are responsible persons, accountable for their own actions and behaviors.

6. Move ahead on the basis of individuals' strengths.

All of us, regardless of our positions, have numerous opportunities to see the good in others and to offer praise. As a manager, a teacher, or a parent we must realize the power of praise and exercise it to its fullest. If we do, we will be bring out the best in those around us, helping them discover their purpose and achieve their full potential. We can begin to "watch our pots." Gradually, they will come to a rolling boil, and to no one's surprise, they will be bubbling over with enthusiasm.

6

Be Enthusiastic

My first priority as superintendent has always been to get out into the schools and visit with students and teachers. One morning as I was walking through a school hall, a teacher came toward me. "Good morning, Mrs. Jones," I greeted her.

"What's good about it?" she grumped.

"It's good because I have this opportunity to look at your beautiful face."

She looked a bit startled, and since I had her attention, I continued in a more down-to-earth vein. "Mrs. Jones, it's good because both of us are looking forward to working with twenty-five very precious people today—you with students, me with teachers. It's exciting to know that we are going to make this day better for them."

She stared at me dubiously.

"Mrs. Jones," I pressed, "did your husband go to work in good health this morning?"

"Yes."

"Did your son go to school?"

"Yes."

"Suzy, your daughter in high school—is she doing okay?"

"Seems to be," she answered.

"Well," I went on, "our principal told me the other day that a few of the girls in the school are pregnant. How about Suzy?"

She looked shocked by my frank inquiry, but she knew what I was getting at.

"She's fine," beamed her mother, smiling with gratitude.

"Well, isn't it a good morning?"

"Absolutely!" she laughed.

Enthusiasm is contagious. It is transmitted from one person to another. But you cannot generate it in others unless you have it yourself.[1]

Ralph Waldo Emerson once said, "Every great and commanding movement in the annals of the world is the triumph of enthusiasm. Nothing great was ever achieved without it."

"Wait a minute," some people will object. "Enthusiasm can be superficial. And besides, we cannot always be enthused, can we?"

True enthusiasm comes from God. In fact, the word is brought over into English from two Greek words: *en* means "in"; *theos* means "God." Literally, *enthusiasm* is "in-God-ism."

Just as it takes only a spark to start a fire, it takes only one enthusiastic person to rouse an entire group of people. Enthusiasm is like the flame of a burning candle that is used to light other candles, to pass on the glow and chase away the darkness. It is like a lighthouse pushing its beam out into the storm to guide people in distress and give hope to those in despair. Benjamin Disraeli stated of enthusiasm, "Every production of genius must be the production of enthusiasm."

How does one go about catching enthusiasm and passing it on? It is really not as elusive as it seems.

Welcome Problems

If we evaluate events in our lives over the past five years, we will recall many situations that seemed to pose insurmountable problems at the time. Yet they turned out to be the opening of doors to excellent opportunities.

When Rubik's Cubes came on the scene a few years ago, most parents bought them for their children. I watched as young people struggled to line up the same color on each of the sides and saw the big, beaming smile radiating success when a child had manipulated more than one side of the same color. I also saw looks of exasperation when they were foiled in the attempt.

Once I asked a parent, "Why do you spend money for a Rubik's Cube when it seems to create such frustration for your child?"

There was a quick response, "I want to present a difficult challenge to my son."

I was impressed with the answer. I believe that though each one of us faces obstacles on the road of life, our attitude toward them determines whether we will consider them problems or challenges. Parents who love their children want them to face realistic, tough challenges in order to reach their fullest potential.

God loves us too, and He will not give us a problem that He knows is beyond our capacity to handle. He does not want us to fail. However, He expects our best efforts.

Check Eroding Enthusiasm

I received a call from a discouraged superintendent of

schools in Ohio. He told me that his teachers had been on strike for several days and had just returned to work. The situation, as he described it, was very tense. I can fully realize the negative impact a teachers' strike can have in a community. It tears apart old relationships, and the spirit of forgiveness and understanding vanishes.

The superintendent, under a great deal of stress, recounted many negative happenings during the strike period. I quickly surmised that he was focusing only on the negatives, blinding himself to the positive side of his leadership. In a word, he had lost his enthusiasm. He was excessively involved in negative talk. I tried to listen to him with patience.

Eventually I asked, "Was any member of your staff, student body, or community physically hurt?"

He said, "Oh, no, it was not that bad."

I inquired again, "Were any of your school buildings vandalized?"

Surprised, he responded, "They would not do anything like that."

I pressed him further, "I hope none of your personal property was damaged."

"Not at all" came the quick reply.

I suggested to him that any of these extreme situations could have happened, but fortunately they did not. "You were the right person in the right spot at the right time," I reminded him. "You may not realize the influence you had personally in keeping these incidents from happening. And while you may not have had any control over the decision to strike, you do have control over the enthusiasm you will radiate as you reach out to renew relationships with your staff."

He agreed.

"Evaluate your situation from a realistic perspective," I told him. "Outline your options and start working with your staff with an open and positive attitude. They may not trust you in the beginning, but you must not let that control your attitude. Do not shortchange yourself with fear and self-pity. Instead, heal the wounds with a genuine caring spirit. Go to your staff with love and understanding. It may seem difficult, but that is what caring is all about. Here is the key: your *enthusiasm* will serve as a catalyst to reunite your teachers and the community."

Our perception of a problem is going to determine the results. If you perceive problems to be bigger than you are, undoubtedly you will surrender to them.

When you feel that you are being overwhelmed by the size of the problem, fight back at once. Take command of your attitude. Approach your problems with faith and calmness and overcome your anxiety. Look at your problem positively and take action on it. If you do, the problem will begin to shrink in size just as an object seems smaller when you look at it through the large end of a pair of binoculars.

Regaining Enthusiasm

One easy way to recapture your enthusiasm is to cancel out the negatives in your life. That's right. Cancel them out. Look instead at the plus side of the ledger. How many times have you caught yourself in such cop-outs as these?

1. "I can't." Of course you can! There really is very little that we are not capable of doing if we put our hearts and minds to it. Persistence and patience will see you through.

2. "It will never work." Of course it will! Maybe not the way you are going about it at the moment, but you can find another way. Who needs a doomsday prophet

in their midst, nipping every dream in the bud? Without our dreamers, we would have missed out on a lot of miracles—like the discovery of America, the first transatlantic flight, or a man on the moon.

3. "It's O.K. as it is." Now, just exactly what does O.K. mean? It means that something is neither great nor terrible. O.K. is mediocre. And we have no time in our lives for mediocrity. Life is too short to major in being average! "So, how are you doing?" "Fine, thanks. I'm feeling great! In fact, magnificent."

4. "I am afraid to try because I may fail." So what? Try, and even if you fail, try again. Trying is better than not trying at all because of fear of failure.

Think of the now famous Alex Haley, the author of the book *Roots*. Was he a sure success with his first attempt at publishing a book? Of course not. In his first eight years of writing he faced many rejection slips and was unable to get a single manuscript published. Yet he was determined, and he maintained enthusiasm in his writing efforts. He was persistent and persevered in order to change his initial failures into a final big success. He continued trying and wrote a best-selling book that was the basis for the most successful TV mini-series in history. He believed in his purpose with enthusiasm.

Our list of negatives could be rather lengthy if we put our minds to it. My point here, however, is not to belabor the enthusiasm squelchers, but to get back to realistic pursuit of legitimate goals. Today begin to cancel out the negatives in your conversations and your personal thoughts. Replace them with these enthusiastic partners: I can. Sure, it will work. That is fantastic! That is magnificent!

Being the bearer of glad tidings is no easy feat in today's society. We seem to be mired down in the negatives. The amusing Murphy's Law, "Whatever can go wrong, will," surrounds us in the world of business, in home management, and even in our personal lives.

B. F. Skinner, the world renowned psychologist and behaviorist, once noted that an athlete is shown again and again the videotapes of his error that lost the game or cost a run, a touchdown, or a yard. Why not show players the moves they do right? he asked. Cancel out the negative by reinforcing the positive.

I noted with interest, and dismay, a recent newsclipping that discussed the stepped-up negative marketing approach in advertising. Advertisers are belittling their competitors and showing what is wrong with their products. We are bombarded with negativism on radio and TV and in the newspapers. In truth, this form of advertising should leave many of us questioning the validity of the product itself.

While enthusiasm is contagious, the lack of it can be, too. Remove yourself from the enthusiasm squelchers. Insulate yourself from the destructive forces that follow a negative thinker. This may seem like drastic action, but if you are really committed to developing your power of positive thinking, you must surround yourself with other enthusiasts. Consider enthusiasm one of our more communicable diseases.

Practice the Faucet Principle

I have a principle I call the "Faucet Principle." Visualize two faucets: one for anxiety, and one for enthusiasm and creativity. You can practice turning off the anxiety faucet and turning on your enthusiasm. The point is that these emotions and behaviors are in your control. Left unattended, one's anxiety faucet tends to run wild and overflow. Our enthusiasm faucet left closed or only partially opened will never reach its full potential and thus never release the abundant energy that lies within us. Enthusiasm toward living helps us to develop positive defenses to help us turn off the anxiety and worry faucet.

Van Varner, *Guideposts* editor, tells a delightful story of a summer drive that he and his godson David were taking in the Rocky Mountains. When they came to a sign that read "Continental Divide," David commented, "This is the great watershed. From here the waters flow either toward the Atlantic or the Pacific."

The remark immediately brought to Varner's mind one of his grandmother's favorite expressions, "watershed moments." She would explain, "In a split second you can often determine which way things are going to go, to the good or to the bad."

Taking Charge

Dr. Viktor Frankl, the bold, courageous psychiatrist who was made a prisoner during the Holocaust, endured years of indignity and humiliation by the Nazis in a concentration camp before he was finally liberated. At the beginning of his ordeal, he was marched into a Gestapo courtroom. His captors had taken away his family, his freedom, and his possessions. His head had been shaved and his body stripped. He had nothing—or did he?

He suddenly realized there was one thing that no one could ever take from him. Can you guess? It was the power to determine his own attitude. "The last of the human freedoms—to choose one's attitude in any given set of circumstances."[2] Bitterness or forgiveness; hatred or hope; determination to endure or the paralysis of self-pity. For every attitude there is its opposite. The choice is ours.

A recent newspaper account by Darrell Sifford of *The Philadelphia Inquirer* titled, "Investing everything in winning—it's a painful road ending in burnout," deals with two football coaches. One is Dick Vermeil who, after his seventh season coaching the Philadelphia Eagles, quit because he said, "I need a break from coaching. The hours I put in have had a draining effect." The other is Tom Landry who, after his twenty-third season with the Dallas Cowboys, still is going strong. Friends say Landry continues to approach the job with freshness and enthusiasm. So why has one burned out, while the other has not?

Dr. Alan L. Summers is a Philadelphia psychiatrist who is the unit medical director at the Northwest Institute of Psychiatry in Illinois. He has never met either of the coaches but, based on what he has read about them and on the patients he has treated, he offers this explanation:

> You take two people with different ego investments. One has the idea that winning is not everything; it's the only thing. He puts himself on the line to such a degree that he can't handle loss because loss becomes personal failure. The psyche takes a battering over losses that are bound to come in a season, and the damage accumulates.

> With the other person, the old-timer, there is the sense that a losing season is part of a learning experience, that things will be better next year. He's able to take an overview and see things over a two- or three-year period.

> If your self-worth depends on having to win all the time, you pay a tremendous price. It seems to me that Landry somehow is able to take a longitudinal view and defeat doesn't destroy who he is.[3]

How does a person avoid that emotional burnout,

whether in his work or in his personal life? Give attention to your re-energizers *before* your emotional well runs dry. Tomorrow is another day, so try again. Cultivate realistic enthusiasm as a primary catalyst in making life's persistently bad situations into good ones.

How to Handle Stress

All of us experience discouraging events at one time or another. The trick in rising above them lies entirely in one's attitude. You have probably heard the expression of Julius Rosewald, then president of Sears Roebuck, "If life gives you a lemon, make lemonade!"

The lemons in our lives all add up to what we call STRESS. It is everywhere. There are books on how to avoid it, how to live with it, how to overcome it, even how to use it effectively. Corporate management is paying particular attention to it, to the tune of millions of dollars annually in an infinite number of "how to manage stress" seminars for their employees.

Stress is not new. And it definitely appears as though it is here to stay. We must discover ways to cope creatively with our own stress if we are to lead well-balanced and mentally healthy lives.

Stress management has also been receiving more and more attention in my field of education in recent years. While the fact that Johnny is caught eating crayons, fighting in the hall, throwing gym equipment on the roof, and releasing small animals, such as frogs, lizards (and once a rabbit) into the classroom, may not seem overly catastrophic, let me assure you—after a time such happenings take their toll on the teacher's psyche!

Morris Weinberger, a professor in the College of Education at Bowling Green State University and an expert on stress management, suggests a three-step approach to coping with stress: (1) Verbalize your feelings; (2) Plan your week to allow for periodic relaxation periods; and (3) Engage in violent exercise, such as racquetball, swimming, or running. Exhaustion is the key, he says.[4]

Dr. Hans Selye, a pioneer in stress studies and an author of over a dozen books and several articles on stress, suggests overcoming an "I-feel-rotten-and-don't-care-about-anything" attitude by taking actions that will make us feel useful. The worst of all stresses, according to Selye, is "purposelessness." Or call it "shifting into neutral." The point is, never by-pass your problems.

I always feel for those young men and women who in their mid-thirties, at their prime of dreaming and accomplishing, talk about looking forward to retirement. It is as if their lives then will be without problems. It is sad that some people at the height of their careers forget what they can do *today*. By always looking to an easier tomorrow, they lack productivity in their present jobs. Life seems to have limited meaning for them.

Life should be a journey, full of stimulating adventures. Sparking every stage of life with enthusiasm will add unique charm and excitement to each day. We need to live exuberantly.

List Your Inspiration Igniters

I have drawn up a list of what I call my "inspiration igniters," helpers I utilize to gain enthusiasm during my low moments. I may choose one or several activities from my list, depending on the dose I need at the time.

Kids are a real inspiration to me. That is one reason that while an administrator, I have always made it a priority to spend time each week in the classroom. These visits help me to see the beautiful smiles, friendship, and love of young people. I hear the candid remarks as well as sense the youthful vibrancy of life. Being in the company of students and teachers is inspiring to me. I feel continuously renewed and uplifted in their company.

By the same token, I often look to my *family* to reactivate my enthusiasm button. Also on my list is *reading* a good book or listening to inspirational *music*. At all costs, I avoid self-pity or the "ain't-it-awfulizing" that is so easy to fall into. I suggest you write out your own list of inspiration igniters and go back and read it the next time your "kettle is low."

Remember, you have a purpose, and with faith the impossible is always possible. Dedication to a purpose will help you to accomplish your goals.

- God will not give you a problem that you cannot handle, because He loves you.
- Look for the pluses and see the good.
- Think of the goals you already have accomplished and those wonderful people who helped you on the way to reach those goals. There are other good people waiting to help you along.
- Keep thinking thoughts of hope and success. Positive talk can help overcome unhappy thoughts.
- Help someone else. You have received much; be willing to give of yourself. You will feel even more useful and needed.
- Look at the beauty and joy of living. Express your gratitude and enjoy your family.
- Go to bed with the thought that you did your best today and be at peace. God will give you another day tomorrow.
- Control your attitude.
- Fill yourself with love.

So you are feeling low? What is your inspiration?

Make your list and be sure to use it next time the negatives threaten you. But remember that winning is not everything. Tackling the defeats are not only learning experiences; they can be inspiring, too.

Remember—Every Problem Has More Than One Solution

Persistence always pays off when one is faced with a problem that appears insurmountable. While I was in Council Bluffs, the school board faced the unpopular decision of canceling the district's sponsorship of the graduation baccalaureate services. A prayer-in-the-school suit ruling that it had lost earlier in the year forced this decision.

Although the first reaction around town was one of anger at being compelled to cancel a fifty-year tradition, parents turned on their creative faucets and came up with some alternatives. One of their first efforts was to contact the city's ministerial association and ask them to sponsor the baccalaureate services. When that failed, a group of parents stepped forward and proceeded to raise over $3,000 in donations to rent a facility and pay a speaker. The response was so strong, they had money left over for the following year! Attendance that year at the alternative baccalaureate was higher than ever, probably because the whole community was involved and had to work hard to carry on the tradition.

Interestingly enough, that year's keynote speaker was former Skylab 4 astronaut Colonel William Pogue. Pogue made it off the ground only after first having had his application to become an astronaut turned down twice and then, once accepted, getting passed over for a couple of missions before finally being chosen. Persistence paid off. Pogue did not give up.

We remember people for their successes, not their failures. Babe Ruth, for example, struck out 1,330 times—more than any other man in baseball history. Yet, we remember his 714 home runs.

Author and Michigan State University professor Eugene Jennings, one of the country's most respected advisors to corporate chairmen and boards, feels that what the executive suite needs today is more people who have failed along the way. Failure, he says, can bring the best out in a true leader. Not that it always does, he adds. But those who fail and then work through their failures and overcome them usually develop an inner strength that is badly needed today.

Says Jennings, "They have the ultimate qualification for leadership today, which is that they've gone through a fire storm of their own making and stayed to put it out."[5] Jennings goes on to state that unlike the sixties, a time when fewer companies lost money or otherwise experienced failure, "We live in a perverse world in which corporate plans and programs fail and jeopardize the firm."[6] He fears that the executives with the "bright, unblemished records" lack essential credentials for dealing with the complex world of the 1980s.

Two Heads Are Better Than One

Are you faced with what seems a defeating problem? Turn on your creative faucet and practice the "two-heads-are-better-than-one" principle.

I have never believed you have to settle a problem alone. Why expend all that energy when you are surrounded by people eager to pick up the ball and run with it? The important thing is to be sure to give them credit for the idea when all is said and done.

Reach Out

What about our role as leaders in motivating others and exposing them to the enthusiasm "bug"? Enthusiasm generates the creative power needed to respond to challenges. By putting the energies generated by our enthusiasm to work and reaching out to others, the possibilities are endless.

Enthusiasm breeds courage. Courage gives people confidence to be willing to change and grow. Given the commonality of all circumstances, individuals with a positive attitude and enthusiasm for life will rise above their difficulties and, as in the case of Viktor Frankl, even survive the cruelties that may come with the territory. A positive attitude will give persons the desire to strive and the will to overcome. Being enthusiastic does not imply that they will have no trials and turmoils; it simply means that they will overcome them with more success than individuals with little or no enthusiasm.

Several college football coaches credited with revitalizing floundering programs they inherited have largely concentrated on bringing about change with positive attitude, enthusiasm, and hard work. Iowa University coach Hayden Fry, George MacIntyre of Vanderbilt, and Bobby Bowden of Florida State have been widely acclaimed for rebuilding their programs over the past five years by using the enthusiasm principle. Explaining how to turn a losing season into a winning one, Fry said, "The first thing you must establish when you go into a losing program is a positive attitude."

In early 1982, I spoke before a civic club. As I was leaving, a young man not much over twenty-five met me at the door. With a somewhat distressed look, he asked if he could talk with me for a minute. I could see that he needed someone to listen. He related the following story.

"A few years ago, I received several thousand dollars from the estate of my parents, and I opened a small retail business. I worked hard and was enthusiastic and optimistic about the future. Soon my business expanded, and eventually I had thirty employees. I began to make diversified investments in apartments and other such properties. I suppose I overstretched myself.

"When the interest rate went above 18 percent in early 1982, I saw my dream shattering as I was losing the gains I had made over the past few years. I became discouraged and lost my enthusiasm. All I had left were failure thoughts that affected my business. After hearing you this noon, I am becoming hopeful. Do you have any suggestions for me?"

I told him I was neither a psychologist nor a financial counselor, but I could raise a few questions for him that might help him to clarify his thinking.

"Do you feel as enthusiastic about your business today as you did when you started out?"

No was the prompt answer.

"Do you feel as positive about the success of your business today as you did a few years ago?"

"No," he replied.

"Do you believe that you can overcome this difficult situation?"

No was the answer again.

"If you had a choice to be in your present situation today when you are young or in your later years, which would you choose?"

"Of course when I am young" was his quick response.

I told him that it seemed to me he needed to outline a plan of action for himself. "First of all," I said, "you must overcome your defeatist attitude and negative thinking. You have to begin to see yourself conquering these temporary setbacks by establishing priorities and tackling them one by one. You need to demonstrate the enthusiasm and faith that you had at the time you started your business. You have to overcome your insecurities.

"Maybe your lack of enthusiasm and your negative thinking are rubbing off on your employees who are not treating your customers with the enthusiasm and the quality of service your customers had come to expect. The source of your trouble is you, but so is the solution. Go on the offensive against these problems, and control your attitude," I suggested to him. "Also, believe that you are tougher than the tough times you are facing. Get busy and overcome your setbacks."

A few months later, my family and I were walking through a furniture store. I saw a well-dressed, enthusiastic-looking man waving and quickly making his way toward us. I recognized the young man as the person with the retail business.

After customary greetings, he told me that he had planned to call me to say how well he was on the road to recovery. I was curious and asked him how he had achieved it.

"After I talked with you, I went home and did some deep analysis of my business," he explained. "I also prayed. I felt more confident and positive about the future. I worked with my financial counselor, rearranged some property ownership, and concentrated on my business. Things are picking up." I could feel the vibrant enthusiasm and his attitude of hope and optimism. I shared in his joy and success.

All of us have opportunities every day to give someone a lift by counting their pluses and building their self-esteem and confidence. Generate the contagious quality of enthusiasm and be a reality thinker. Think about what you have rather than what you do not have. Count your advantages rather than the disadvantages. Plan your priorities.

As I mentioned earlier, whenever I feel less than enthusiastic, I visit a school. Once in one of the classes I met a severely handicapped preschooler who always gave me a big, happy smile. She had no legs or arms. I saw her rolling in the hall like a little ball, which was her "happy walk." She insisted that she make her own way rather than being carried. I saw her persistence in feeding herself. This little four year old never indicated that she felt sorry for herself. She inspired me and renewed my enthusiasm for life. She had learned early in life the power of realistic thinking and sharing enthusiasm. She always made me grateful about what I have and what I am able to do.

If you are a manager, look for inspiration igniters. Watch for good work on the part of your staff, and compliment them enthusiastically. If you are a clerk, be courteous and caring and treat your customers with respect. Be enthused over the fact that they trade with you. If you are a teacher, be enthusiastic about your students and their abilities. At home, make sure your family members know that they are needed and respected and that they make your life joyous and worthwhile.

Your enthusiasm is just one more factor in making bad situations good, and it places you one step closer to achieving the best in life.

7

Expect the Best

On my first visit to a classroom in Council Bluffs, I was impressed by the inquisitive young faces I saw there. Were these the same children who had ranked so low on test scores? They did not look any different from students I had seen in other cities. In fact, they looked very intelligent to me. I decided to tell them so.

"I want you all to know that I think you are among the brightest children I have met," I said. "I'm proud to be associated with you." As I told them how certain I felt that they would do exceedingly well in the coming year, I saw a look of expectancy brighten their faces.

When the teacher walked out into the hall with me, I said, "I noticed your fine rapport with the children and how well they respond to you." Shaking her hand, I added, "I know you're going to do great things with them."

I am not talking here about a Pollyanna-type philosophy. In telling my teachers that I appreciate their skills, I am also letting them know that I expect the best from them. "We will help you to grow," I tell them. "But if you cannot grow, we will help you find satisfaction in some other job."

We found that 90 percent of the teachers were doing well. Most of the rest were surprised when we frankly told them they were not. "No one has told me that for ten years," said one. "What am I doing wrong? I'll try to correct it." These people we were able to help.

For the few who were obviously not designed to be teachers in the first place, we helped them see this reality and then assisted them in finding vocations elsewhere in which they could be productive and happy.[1]

The key to almost any successful organization, whether it is a family unit, a major corporation, or a rural high school, is found in happy employees who are proud of their organization and who strive for high productivity. And both factors require expecting the best. This is the glue that binds things together.

Weaving in and out of the tapestry of any successful organization is the matter of attitude. I happen to believe that by expecting the best, we will not only achieve the impossible for ourselves but also will inspire others to greater heights along the way. Such an attitude is contagious. Developing this powerful attitude requires diligence and practice, but the rewards are endless.

Wilma Rudolph, born a sickly child, eventually went on to win three gold medals in track events at the 1960 Olympics in Rome. At the age of four, she had scarlet fever and double pneumonia that left her badly crippled. The doctors predicted that some day she would probably be able to walk again—but only with the aid of crutches. Undeterred by the doctors' prognosis, Wilma always responded to questions about what she was going to do when she grew up by saying she was going to run in the Olympics. She was determined, and she fully expected to overcome her disability.

Wilma received help from her brother Wesley who served as her coach, helped her with exercises, and continually encouraged her. He taught her how to dribble and shoot a basketball. Always he expressed his positive expectations of her. Little by little, strength came to her crippled limbs. Then one day her mother looked out the kitchen window and, to her happy surprise, saw Wilma running around without her leg brace on.

Wilma went on to receive a basketball scholarship at a large southern university. She never forgot the early pronouncements of her doctors that she might be able to walk some day with crutches. Her determination, hard work, and self-imposed expectation to be a runner made her a winner—the first American woman to win three gold medals in the Olympics. She was named America's outstanding amateur athlete by the Amateur Athletic Union.

Wilma's road was full of obstacles. Her determination, her faith, and her expectations of herself, supported by the encouragement of her brother and mother, gave her the power to tolerate and overcome the pain and suffering involved in reaching her goal.

Anyone can overcome defeat by following the simple guideline of expecting the best. It is a matter of conditioning the mind and heart in positive directions.

Analyze Your Choices

Many ways exist of overcoming the obstacles that prevent your attaining the best, no matter how insurmountable those obstacles may seem. Ignoring problems is not a wise course, however. Left to themselves they do not go away; they only compound.

I set out to tackle problems by first seeing the opportunities in them. Every problem has genuine opportunities hidden somewhere in it. Like diagramming a sentence in grammar class, I sometimes begin with paper and a pencil when facing a difficulty. I ask myself, What is good about this situation? What are my choices to turn this dilemma around? I put the issues down in black and white. Soon suitable options begin to emerge, and prioritizing them leads to a plan of action.

When I began my first principalship, the school, as I mentioned earlier, was plagued by discipline problems. Parents and community were extremely critical of the poor image of the school. At the same time, teachers were overburdened with numerous supervisory tasks. My opportunities list ran something like this:

1.   The students are basically fine; they just need supervision.

2.   The teachers' overloaded schedules could be relieved if a volunteer force would assume some of the supervisory tasks in the school, such as playground, lunch room, and bus stop.

3.   Parents in the community are critical only because they are interested in seeing the situation improve. At worst, they could be apathetic.

4.   A newly formed Parent-Teacher Association was enthusiastic and eager to participate in school projects.

As you can readily see, a solution was quickly rising to the surface as I examined my list. Item four was the key. The outcome?

The Parent-Teacher Association enlisted parents to assist with the supervisory duties. The result was that parents had a new understanding of the administrative problems in a school setting. In addition, they were able to observe their children in a different social environment. Teachers' morale improved because they had time for planning ahead.

And the discipline problems? They were reduced drastically. People focused their creative energies on developing alternatives that would lead to solutions rather than blaming each other and the school for problems.

If you generally begin by expecting the worst, here are a few easy exercises to help reshape your thinking.

1. *Look in the mirror and verbally count your strengths.* Activate your positive emotions by saying, "Good things can start happening to me." Visualize your fears draining from your mind and, at the same time, new positive thoughts taking their place. Remember— fear is the darkroom where negatives are developed! Positive thoughts produce good feelings.

2. *Give your best to your job, your family, and your community, and the best will come back to you.* You must put your heart and soul into your efforts in order to achieve the anticipated results. "Putting your heart into it" implies stretching yourself, like a rubberband, to your fullest extent. We really do reap what we sow. Give of yourself fully and totally. Maintain the highest commitment to your goal.

3. *Believe in yourself and your dreams.* People from unexpected and unknown sources will help you. Do not allow failure to obscure your goals. Your faith and perseverance will make the difference. Free yourself of your doubts, and fill your mind with success thoughts.

4. *Watch your attitude and expectations.* Your attitude has a mirroring effect on others.

I met a retired professor in one city whose talents, abilities, and prior experiences were outstanding. He had served not only as a professor but also as a college president, and he had held many prestigious positions in the field of education. He told me one day of an incident that happened to him many years before.

He was assigned for a second time to teach a particular course to senior students. "Teaching this course," he said, "was a drudgery because students hated the subject matter. It was a discouraging situation, and I dreaded the very thought of it. The fact is, it was becoming more and more an emotional issue for me. One summer day I sat down to analyze why the students didn't like this course. Why did they feel bored and uninspired?"

The long analysis, according to this professor, revealed something he had never thought of before. He simply did not like teaching the course; he had no enthusiasm for it. First he had to change his attitude about the situation. Then he got busy and rewrote his teaching syllabus from this new perspective.

"The next semester," my friend said, "was so much more exciting. Students responded to the course with enthusiasm. I enjoyed teaching it. By changing my attitude, I was able to change my students' response."

5. *Write down on index cards your own positive thoughts, including quotations from your favorite inspirational authors.* Refer to the Bible—both Old and New Testaments—for inspiration and uplift. Fill your mind with happy thoughts and clear it of failure thoughts. The latter generate fear, which in turn inhibits the flow of your creativity. Rejuvenate your energy by putting your mind, heart, and body to work. Think good thoughts. Believe in your heart that the impossible is possible, and let those thoughts seep into your mind. Believing good things will happen to you is vital to their becoming a reality.

6. *Know when and where you want to be at a certain point in your life.* Then put your whole self into accomplishing that goal.

7. *Be yourself.* Do not try to behave in a manner that is not at all like your real self. Your efforts to show in your behavior what you actually are not will hamper your efforts to reach your goal.

Pursuit of Joy

Someone once asked Will Rogers, "If you had just forty-five days left in which to live, how would you live them?"

"One at a time" was Rogers's reply.

If overcoming the negatives in your life seems to be an overwhelming task, tackle them one at a time. Again, your best method will be to accentuate the positive.

A close family friend describes her life's philosophy as a determined pursuit of joy. I can attest to this woman's vibrant enthusiasm for life and her unending concern for others. She is an active volunteer on behalf of the schools and numerous civic organizations. To find joy, she says, one must observe it, seek it, and give it. Each day she tries to fill her mind with caring by observing others' kindnesses and by offering her own good deeds. The practice, she claims, keeps her mind on positive thoughts.

While I was living in Ohio, I learned of a remarkable woman named Edna Crisman, a resident of the village of Delta. She served elaborate five-course dinners in her home, using her best china and sterling silverware. Reservations for these meals were in great demand. At the time she was over eighty-five, but she seemed to serve her customers with a great deal of satisfaction.

My curiosity got the best of me, and I asked a friend to explain how Mrs. Crisman had come to host these fabulous dinners in her home. It seemed the woman's husband owned a hardware store that incurred losses during the Great Depression and had difficulty meeting its expenses. So at the age of fifty-two she decided to augment the family income by serving fancy dinners. She enjoyed it so much and was such an excellent cook that she kept up the practice even after the financial crisis had passed. Citizens in the area liked to celebrate their special days by reserving a dinner cooked with such special care by this lady.

She began her endeavor in order to meet a need, but her enjoyment in service to others motivated her to continue her practice. Now at age ninety-five, Mrs. Crisman still serves meals with the help of some local high school students.

The village council of Delta, showing its love and esteem for the founder of the "Hostess House," on her ninety-fifth birthday—November 11, 1983—proclaimed "Edna Crisman Week." An article in the local newspaper described her as the "Queen of Delta" and stated, "She has given her love and courage to every one who has come in contact with this most gracious and beautiful lady."[2] To Mrs. Crisman, her customers are her family.

Mrs. Crisman faced and overcame the disasters of her life, including the closing of her husband's business, the complete breakdown of his health, and the earlier responsibility of the support of her widowed mother. Edna Crisman found the good in all these difficult situations. She assessed her strengths and made the most of them.

Edna Crisman, a regular churchgoer, never lost her faith in God to help her overcome adversities. Her zest for living and the satisfaction she finds in her work keep her going at age ninety-five. Retirement? She says, "If I can keep on walking, I can keep on working."[3] This is an example of a purposeful life full of faith and service.

At the age of eight Glenn Cunningham, a Kansas farm boy, suffered severe burns to his legs in an accident. The limbs were so badly damaged that the doctors advised amputation. But Glenn and his parents determined instead to undertake the seemingly impossible by trying to save his limbs. A demanding regimen of exercise was set up, and his parents massaged his legs by the hour.

When Glenn was eventually able to walk with crutches, his friends, seeing him outside for the first time since the accident, stopped playing, knowing he was unable to join in their running games. But Glenn did not want their pity and encouraged them to continue their play. Some day, he said, he would beat them. After four years of exercising and massaging, Glenn's legs were greatly improved. The doctors suggested he try running to further strengthen them.

So Glenn ran. And he ran. His parents, who never lost hope, were reaping rewards for their faith and determination. In turn, they poured words of encouragement into Glenn's mind and heart, assuring the young boy that he could do it. At thirteen, Glenn was able to beat his playmates in running. He had not given up, and the impossible had been realized.

When Glenn entered the University of Kansas at Lawrence, his track coach became familiar with his courage and determination. He predicted that Glenn would become one of the greatest runners in the history of track. As a senior, he ran the mile in 4 minutes 6.7 seconds—a new world record at the time. He represented the United States in the Olympic Games at Los Angeles and Berlin in 1932 and 1936, respectively. Glenn's achievements were the product of high expectation coupled with determination and perseverance.

The Power of High Expectations

Teachers who aim for the best and believe that their students will succeed are, indeed, setting those children on a high-achievement track. Conversely, teachers who have a low opinion of their students' abilities generally guarantee these children's failures.

In Act V of George Bernard Shaw's *Pygmalion,* Eliza Doolittle explains to Colonel Pickering:

> You see, really and truly, apart from the things anyone can pick up (the dressing and the proper ways of speaking, and so on), the difference between a lady and a flower girl is not how she behaves, but how she's treated. I shall always be a flower girl to Professor Higgins, because he always treats me as a flower girl, and always will; but I know I can be a lady to you, because you always treat me as a lady, and always will.

Interestingly enough, this same "Pygmalion effect" applies not only to flower girls but also consistently reappears in the classroom, in management, and in the context of marriage and family relationships. It is not so much a matter of "what you see is what you get" but of "what you expect is what you get."[4]

Some executives manage their employees in a way that leads to superior performance. However, others, like Professor Higgins, unintentionally manage in a way that leads to their subordinates' performing below their achievement capabilities.

So, what makes a good manager good or a bad manager bad? The key, according to most researchers, lies in their level of realistic expectation of their employees.

An excellent example of this phenomenon was noted in a large West Coast bank where, with few exceptions, the most effective branch managers were men in their forties and fifties. The bank managers believed much time was needed to develop appropriate background knowledge to handle the responsibilities of the job.

One exception, however, was a twenty-seven-year-old branch manager who ranked in the top 10 percent of the managers according to effectiveness. He had been promoted to his position at age twenty-five, and in two years he not only improved the performance of his bank considerably but also contributed to the development and growth of his younger assistant so that he, in turn, was made a branch manager at twenty-five.

This man had been only an average student in college, but in his first four years at the bank, he had the good fortune to be assigned to work with two branch managers who were remarkably effective teachers. It is significant that his first boss, who was recognized throughout the bank for his exceptional skill in developing young recruits, did not believe that it took years to gain the knowledge and skill necessary to become an effective banker.[5]

Case studies reveal that a unique characteristic of superior managers is their ability to create high performance expectations in their subordinates. Less effective managers fail to develop similar expectations, resulting in lower productivity. Subordinates, more often than not, appear to do what they believe they are expected to do.[6]

Research has also established that, in educational settings, these self-fulfilling prophecies consistently demonstrate that teachers' expectations are very effective in influencing achievement and growth in younger children. The same conclusions were drawn in terms of a young adult's first experience with a manager. A first manager is likely to be the most influential person in that individual's career.[7]

The implications of this research can very well be applied to a family setting. Consider the influence we have as parents or as spouses on those with whom our relationships are closest. Virginia Satir, author of *Peoplemaking,* voices this concern in the question, "Are you tending their pots?"

Setting high standards is not enough. We must have

high expectations and a definite game plan for reinforcement when those expectations are met, but we also need a strategy if the expectations are not met. The best investment an organization can make is in the growth of its employees, which can be sustained by staff development efforts, constant praise, constructive criticism of behavior, and emotional support. People in such organizations will show pride and high productivity.

Consistency Counts

I was a guest recently of one of the major hotel chains, and after meetings one afternoon I retreated to one of those delightful, bubbling hot tubs. Three young children joined me, evidently on vacation with their family. Their mother appeared on the scene and said it was time for the children to come out and dress for dinner. The request went unheeded, and five minutes later she returned to repeat her command. When this, too, was ignored, her voice became more forceful. "You kids get out of there right now. I'm going to count to five and I want you out of there, or else!"

By now, the scenario was becoming quite familiar, and I figured I could almost write its ending.

"One...two...three...," she counted.

Two of the children popped up out of the tub and headed for their room.

"Four...," she continued. The third child was obviously enjoying this counting game. He grinned at me.

"Five!" the mother concluded. "That's it, now you get out of there and come get dressed!" With that, she turned and marched off to the room.

I could not believe it. One of the first rules in disciplining is that once you have made your expectations known, you must follow through. And then you must be consistent. In *The One Minute Manager,* Kenneth Blanchard, Ph.D., and Spencer Johnson, M.D., succinctly spell out the importance of following through with one-minute reprimands when required. "Goals begin behaviors," they write. "Consequences maintain behaviors."

By the same token, unrealistically high expectations can result in distress when applied without compassion. When our oldest son, Dick, was seven years old he struggled with a speech problem. My wife and I were constantly correcting him and, admittedly, losing our patience in the process.

About this same time he began sleepwalking, a habit we learned later was an outcome of his inability to meet our expectations. It was not until his fourth-grade teacher, a beautiful, caring woman, took him aside and worked with him that his sleepwalking disappeared. So, too, did his speech problem. We learned an important lesson on how to encourage and be positive in our support.

Management research and family psychology have long pointed out the need for parents to establish goals together and then follow through with the supervision and application of praise and criticism as required. I offer the following suggestions for applying the expect-the-best principle at your place of work or in your family:

1.   Clearly define the expectations in a precise, easily understood manner.

2.   Be sure that the criteria for measuring success are thoroughly comprehended and agreed upon to maintain proper accountability.

3.   Show trust in the abilities and talents of the person or persons to produce the anticipated results.

4.   Be supportive and encouraging, not nagging or intruding.

5. Offer praise, suggestions, and reinforcement at appropriate intervals.

6. Be optimistic about seeing your dreams come true.

While I was completing my doctorate at Bowling Green State University in 1970, I attended the Ohio School Boards Capital Conference. I remember taking a seat in the back of the convention hall filled with over four thousand educators and board members from across the state. Listening to the keynote speaker, I recall thinking, *I want to be there someday, addressing these professionals.*

In November 1982, my dream was fulfilled when Craig Gifford, executive vice president of the association, invited me to be the keynote speaker at the convention. By expecting the best, by listening to your dreams, you become receptive to the many opportunities that flow your way. But responsibility accompanies each opportunity.

Expecting the Best Demands the Best

Life is a lot like a bank account: you can take out only what you put in.

Expecting the best requires a willingness to put forth your best efforts. As a young boy, I remember my grandmother's periodically carrying a twenty-five to thirty pound bag of wheat to the mill a half mile away to have it ground into flour. When I grew older, she enlisted my back to carry the load to and from the mill. She marched at my side.

I recall sometimes saying, "Oh, let's not do it today, Grandmother. I'm tired. I've worked hard in school all day. Let's go tomorrow."

Her usual reply was, "I've never seen anyone die of hard work, but I've seen people die of laziness."

In June 1983, the Shawnee Mission School District and the North Kansas City, Missouri, School District cohosted the annual conference of the National Association of Student Councils, which is sponsored by the National Association of Secondary School Principals. It was attended by over thirteen hundred student leaders and faculty advisors from all over the United States. Their theme for the weeklong convention was "Leadership Begins in the Heart."

Through the duration of the conference, I observed these students grappling with such challenging issues as prayer in public schools, a national minimum age of twenty-one for drinking alcoholic beverages, and the viability of a freeze on the development of nuclear weapons. The air was literally charged with the energy, enthusiasm, and vitality of these young people.

As I considered the impact these leaders would soon have on our nation, I felt my own thoughts turning to hope and to great expectations. By calling for the best, I had at least a part in molding these kids to do the same.

Those young adults were making, and will make in the future, a difference in our tumultuous environment. Already they had grasped the significance of purpose in life, and their purpose was unique and powerful. They *will* make a difference!

And so will the people who respond to your expectations.

8

Determine to Make a Difference

History sparkles with the names of people who have believed they could effect changes in their world. These people make a difference wherever they are and whatever their sphere of influence. They have the courage to dare and to dream and are willing to take the risks to realize their dreams. They also inspire others to a commitment to a worthy goal, a new idea, and sometimes a departure from tradition.

In 1960 the late President John F. Kennedy challenged the nation to land the first man on the moon by the end of the decade. His ringing challenge was transformed into a collective vision for the whole nation. He raised the aspirational level of not only his own countrymen but also of the whole world. The energies and the efforts of the entire nation focused on this common vision—to make America first on the moon.

That vision was realized on July 20, 1969, when the whole world watched in awe as Neil Armstrong stepped triumphantly on the moon and said, "That's one small step for man, one giant leap for mankind." It was a proud moment for every American. The task of landing a man on the moon was accomplished in the American pioneer spirit.

Behind the scenes, there were many dedicated, though virtually unknown, scientists, engineers, technologists, and other workers who made a positive difference in the success of that climactic mission and the ones leading up to it. The ability of a leader to dream and then inspire a nation to believe in that vision made the difference.

Making Them Winners

Jaime Escalante, a native of Bolivia, immigrated to the United States in 1964. Escalante worked hard to learn English and to receive a college degree in mathematics and electronics. He began working for the Burroughs Corporation as a technician. His first love, however, was teaching. So in 1974, at a reduced salary, he made a career change and became a math teacher in Garfield High, an inner city school in Los Angeles.

In the summer of 1982, the educational world was dumfounded when all eighteen of Escalante's students taking the advanced-placement (AP) calculus examination passed the test, with seven scoring the highest possible marks.

Escalante brought to his teaching a blend of two important techniques: (1) raising the aspirational level of students, and (2) demanding hard work from them at school and at home. He reached out to students with encouragement but maintained his high expectations. "You are winners," he repeated to them. He made himself available to his students before and after school and throughout the summer months.

An article by Randy Fitzgerald in the August 1983 edition of *Reader's Digest* described Escalante's method of inspiring his students: "Calculus is just a name to you right now," he told them, "but when I get through, you'll all be champs. Do what's expected of you, and I'll do what's expected of me. There are no limits. You can become whatever you want to be." His classroom walls were plastered with such motivational signs as "Determination + Discipline + Hardwork = The Way to Success."

The Educational Testing Service in Princeton, which did the testing, not fully realizing the impact this dedicated and giving teacher had on his students in inspiring them to learn, had some reservations. "The results did not make sense" to the testing service. Confidently believing in his teaching methods and maintaining great faith in his students, Jaime Escalante agreed to have them retake the test. On August 31, 1982, twelve of the students repeated the test. All twelve were successful in passing the examination, each with the highest possible score.

Any teacher who loves both teaching and students is bound to make a difference in the lives of his or her pupils. Escalante brought the best out in each one of them. He did not accept the modern statement that inner city students cannot achieve. He was not burdened by lack of expectation. All they needed was to be inspired by example, and Jaime Escalante provided that generously. There are scores of other such teachers who, like the little known support crew in a successful space mission, are making a positive difference in the lives of their students and, through them, humanity.

I know a teacher in one of the Shawnee Mission high schools who, though confined to a wheelchair, always wears a big smile and reaches out to staff and students alike. Students love and respect this woman for her dedication and enthusiasm for life.

I recall another teacher in Ohio who is a victim of multiple sclerosis. During my two-year tenure at the school, I saw her limp grow worse until she eventually began walking with a cane. She is now in a powerdriven wheelchair that she calls "Amigo." I knew then and I know now that this teacher is an inspiration to all. She focuses not on her handicaps but on her purpose to serve and inspire youth. Yes, these teachers make a difference in the lives of their students. Because of their sense of purpose, life for them is a joyous experience.

A Miracle Worker's Personal Victory

All of us know about Helen Keller, the deaf and blind child, famed for her remarkable achievements in overcoming her handicaps. But do you know the background of the remarkable "miracle worker" Anne Sullivan, her teacher, whose unlimited patience, perseverance, and purposefulness helped Helen Keller to overcome her handicaps?

Anne Sullivan's own childhood was marred with partial blindness due to trachoma so that she could see only shadows of figures. She lived with an alcoholic father and frequently suffered from his beatings when he was under the influence. Her mother was bedridden with tuberculosis, but she always encouraged Anne to be thankful. Her mother died when Anne was not yet eight years old. Her brother and sister, Jimmie and Mary, went to live with their father's brother, while Anne remained with her father to do the household chores.

When Anne's uncle realized she was often abused, he brought her to live with them. His wife, however, felt Anne was a bad influence on their other children, and she insisted that the girl be sent to Tewksbury, an institution described by Anne Sullivan's uncle as a place for "the sick, the insane, the criminals, the defeated, the lowest scum."[1] She was sent there along with her brother Jimmie who died a few months later.

After staying for over three years at Tewksbury, she

was sent to Perkins Institution for the Blind. At the age of thirteen, she had not yet learned to read, and the other students often laughed at her because of this deficiency. But she eventually found a caring person in Sophia Hopkins, the matron of the school. During summer vacations Mrs. Hopkins took Anne to her home on Cape Cod where the girl learned to swim. The kind, sympathetic attitude of Sophia Hopkins brought about a great change in the young girl.

Anne began to work hard at her studies, and by the time of her graduation she was class valedictorian. Trying on her new clothes for the graduation ceremonies, Anne looked at herself in the mirror and said, "I'm beautiful!"[2] Mrs. Hopkins smiled and responded, "You certainly are."

The emergence of her new, inner strength was obvious when as valedictorian, Anne spoke to her fellow graduates:

> Today we are standing face to face with the greatest problems of life. We have spent years in the endeavor to acquire the moral and intellectual discipline by which we are enabled to distinguish truth from falsehood, receive higher and broader views of duty, and apply general principles to the diversified details of life. And now we are going out into the busy world, to take our share in life's burdens, and do our little to make the world better, wiser, and happier.[3]

She concluded her remarks with the challenge,

> Fellow graduates, duty bids us go forth into an active life. Let us go cheerfully, hopefully, and earnestly and set ourselves to find our special part. When we have found it, willingly and faithfully perform it; for every obstacle we overcome, every success we achieve tends to

bring man closer to God and makes life more as He would have it.[4]

This girl had suffered the scars of an unfortunate childhood, the pain of institutional life, numerous operations on her eyes, cruel jokes from her classmates, and even the threat of being expelled from school by the administration. But finally the love of Matron Sophia Hopkins came into her life at a time when Anne's troubles seemed endless.

On March 20, 1887, she wrote to Mrs. Hopkins concerning her work with Helen Keller,

> My heart is singing for joy this morning. A miracle has happened! The light of understanding has shone upon my little pupil's mind, and behold, all things are changed. The great step—the step that counts—has been taken. The little savage has learned her first lesson in obedience, and finds the yoke easy. It now remains my pleasant task to direct and mold the beautiful intelligence that is beginning to stir in the child's soul.[5]

Annie Sullivan died in October 1936, but only after helping Helen Keller overcome her handicaps and achieve phenomenal success—and bringing her closer to God. She kept her promise.

You Never Know!

Each one of us has the opportunity to make a difference in the lives of others. You never know who you may be influencing right now. The true success of a man or a woman should not be measured in the end only by the wealth accumulated, or the position reached, but by the service rendered, the obstacles overcome, the perseverance demonstrated, the courage displayed, and the special part played in making the world a better place.

Each of us has been touched in lasting ways by people who cared enough to reach out and make a difference in our own lives.

The magic power of a teacher's touch continues in thousands of classrooms even today. A teacher in one of the Shawnee Mission elementary schools in October 1983 received this letter, which reflects on the lasting influence of a caring teacher.

Dear Mr. Green:

I just wanted to share a little something with you. I was thinking maybe teachers don't hear often enough about when they've done something really wonderful!

Since last year, we have had many small battles over M's extreme reluctance to begin reading. We have been very upset over this for such a long time, as my husband and myself are avid readers. Rather than make such an issue of it this year we decided to just lay low and hope he would change his attitude. So far this year I hadn't seen any improvement and I could just see the whole business starting all over again.

You can imagine my surprise and delight when yesterday M brought home *Magic Afternoon* and proceeded to sit down and read the entire book to me! I was absolutely thrilled. I had no idea the child could read since he has emphatically refused to do so in the past. When I asked him why he decided to start reading he said, "So Mr. Green will be proud of me."

Whatever your "magic" is, we are very grateful for it! I just feel so positive about M's new success I wanted you to know.

Thank you, thank you!

Jeanne E. Lane

Those Who Made the Difference

History is filled with stories of people who refused to accept visible limitations and *believed they could make a positive difference.*

Louis Braille, born January 4, 1809, in Coupvray, France, the son of a saddler is one such example. Louis became blind at age three in an accident while he was trying to punch a hole in some leather in his father's workshop. His doctor announced to the Brailles after several weeks of treatment, "I am deeply sorry, but in all probability, your son will never see again."

Most blind persons at that time became beggars. Not wanting this to happen, the boy's parents sent him to the National Institute for the Blind located in Paris. He was given his lessons, using an embossed letter technique that was the prevailing system for teaching reading to the blind. Because of the large size of the letters and the resulting tremendous cost of production, reading material was extremely limited. Braille did not like the embossing system because it made the reading process quite slow.

In April 1821, Charles Barbier, a retired army captain, visited the institute and presented his system called "night-writing," which used an arrangement of raised dots. His system was originally designed to communicate code messages in the military. Twelve-year-old Louis Braille was fascinated with this system, and he began experimenting with raised dots on his own. He faced many discouragements and failures as he worked to refine letters and numbers into a dot system. He had hope for the blind if he could only perfect the method.

Braille worked diligently, often late into the night. But his progress was so slow he thought of quitting. About that time, Valentin Hauy, the founder of the institute, returned to Paris following extended efforts to start schools for the blind in other parts of the world. At age seventy-six, he was to receive a special tribute from the institute.

Hauy, in addressing the students, said with deep emotion,

> From the very beginning, I have hoped this school would be a bright torch held aloft to bring light to the blind. Those of you who are here this evening are now the custodians of this torch. I beg of you, guard it carefully. You must carry it to the legions of your fellows who still live in darkness....I have wanted neither honor nor fortune for my own feeble efforts. The only reward I wish is the knowledge that the light we have created here, with God's help, will spread until it illuminates the life of the last blind man on this earth.[6]

Little could Hauy know that what he said that day was to change the course of history for the blind worldwide. Hauy's message touched young Louis Braille who felt as though the torch had been passed personally to him. His attitude changed from discouragement to determination, from preoccupation with failure to success. He redoubled his efforts to refine his dot system. By age fifteen, he developed a workable alphabet. Two years later he became an assistant teacher at the institute, and after his graduation he agreed to remain there as a professor. By 1826, he had further perfected his dotted alphabet which we know today as the Braille system.

His system was not immediately accepted by the government, although students in the institute showed a high level of enthusiasm for it. The saddler's son, who brought a new light for the blind in every part of the world, died on January 6, 1852, without realizing the full impact his system would have on the world in the years to come. But he did not do it alone.

Charles Barbier made the first impact in the life of the twelve-year-old boy. He lit the spark, and when it nearly flickered out, Hauy came along to fan it into full flame. His inspiring comments made the difference for Louis at a crucial time when the young man was ready to quit. In turn, Louis Braille brought the world's great literature to the blind everywhere.

You Can Make the Difference

Most teachers are making a difference for their pupils. An example is this letter that I received from a parent:

Dear Dr. Chopra:

May I take a moment of your time to tell you about a very valuable teacher you have on your staff.

Our daughter, Helen, had the good fortune to be in one of Mary Frances Hodgson's science classes. Miss Hodgson made the subject so alive that Helen would come home and enthusiastically relate to us what she had learned that day in science class. This excellent teacher kindled a spark of undying love for the subject in that little girl with the result that after her own children were in school Helen continued her education and will receive a Ph.D. in bio-chemistry from the University of Notre Dame next March. She has been accepted for two years of postdoctoral study at the University of Washington after which she plans to do research.

Our family is so grateful to Miss Hodgson and deeply thankful that Helen was fortunate enough to be one of her students. The influence of such a wonderful teacher is immeasurable.

Sincerely,

Josephine and William Spidell

Mother Teresa, born on August 27, 1910, in Skopje, Yugoslavia, is called "Mother" in India—the highest tribute any Indian can pay. She, too, has made a difference for mankind. At the age of eighteen, she left her home in order to become a nun, eventually being sent to India.

Touched by the suffering and poverty of many people in Calcutta, Mother Teresa became convinced that her role was not in education dealing with middle class people but among the "poorest of the poor." She found her avenue of service in the slums where people die without anybody in attendance, and where leprosy victims are pushed away by their own relatives or asked to commit suicide.

Mother Teresa's call to work with the poor and sick was further affirmed after the partition of India in 1947, which sent millions of refugees fleeing from Pakistan to India. Mother Teresa established her center in Calcutta to serve them.

In 1949, while searching for a home in which to locate her mission, she wrote: "Today I learned a good lesson. The poverty of the poor must be so very hard for them. While looking for a home, I walked and walked until my arms and legs ached. I thought how much they must ache in body and in soul looking for a home, food, health."[7] Mother Teresa, by reaching out with love, has provided dignity for human beings even in death. "How many times we have picked people up from the street who have lived like animals and long to die like angels," she said. The Missionaries of Charity have provided hope for the hopeless, food for the hungry, homes for the homeless, love for the unloved, and care for the neglected.

Mother Teresa has fulfilled the commandment of "love thy neighbor" in its truest form. She and her associates have chosen to see the good in every human being and provide them dignity in life and death. Mother Teresa is making the difference for thousands of people throughout the world with the work she started in Calcutta. She describes this work as responding to "the will of God." She stated so beautifully, "We can do no great things—only small things with great love."

Branch Rickey, one-time general manager of the Brooklyn Dodgers, has been credited by many commentators as being the one who provided the momentum to make baseball the game it is today. Branch Rickey brought Jackie Robinson, the first black, into professional baseball. Rickey knew at the time the possible humiliation Jackie might have to bear from various sources. He took time to talk with him and to prepare him for the setbacks so that Jackie could focus on his talents, look to the future, and prove himself as the first black major league baseball player. Branch Rickey made a difference, using his courage to break tradition and to give that chance to Jackie Robinson. And, yes, Jackie Robinson made a difference in the annals of baseball and proved himself worthy. He opened doors for other blacks to enter the major leagues.

Four Specific Ways to Make a Difference

History continues to be repeated by people who are making a difference in the lives of others by raising their aspirational level. How easy it is for most of us to think that we make little difference in this big world. But in any organization, capable people are found who are like the unsung heroes of the space program working behind the scenes, making the difference between the success and the failure of a mission. Here are ways to help you make a difference:

1. *Say no to a fear of failure.* The fault is not in failing but in quitting when we fail. The real failure lies in not doing what needs to be done because we are afraid to take risks. We too often want to play it safe. An Italian proverb reflects this philosophy: *"Chi non risica, non rosica."* This means, "He who does not take a chance will never have a bone to nibble and chew."

2. *Give of yourself.* Learn to be a servant, not a taker. This means serving your community, your organization, and your church for neither acclaim nor accolades. Improve the quality of life around you and give joy to others.

3. *Find your special place, your niche.* Everyone has an important role to play in a society. I know of a young man, Joe, who suffers from cerebral palsy, but he has found his own special part. He knew he could not play basketball so he chose to become the manager of his high school basketball team. In his words, "That was the closest thing to being in the game."

With the right attitude he found his special part. According to the coach of the team, "He gave 100 percent at whatever he did."

How did the basketball team feel about him? During special pregame celebrations, seniors on the team presented their moms corsages. As this young manager of the team stepped on the court to pin the corsage on his mother, the team members, students, and spectators gave them a standing ovation. This young manager played his part, and they applauded him because he made a difference for the team by his service and caring. He found his niche.

If a motorist is stuck on the highway, he needs an auto mechanic, not a doctor. Similarly a patient in the emergency room is relieved to see a doctor. Every person has a special place in this world.

4. *Persevere toward your goals.* Learn to finish what you start, and finish with excellence, with "class." Never settle for mediocrity. Challenge half-hearted efforts wherever you find them.

Indeed, we *can* make a difference in our own lives and in the lives of others. We need always to remember that we are not alone, for our families and our friends can be strong pillars of support for us. Let us nurture and celebrate these relationships because we do need each other. Together we can make a difference.

9

Love and Laugh

In our endeavor to improve bad situations, two aspects of management are often overlooked. They are the two very human elements of love and laughter.

As leaders, we are told that our task is to organize, delegate, and supervise. We are given *Robert's Rules of Order.* We are instructed to dress for success. And that is fine. But we also need to be lovers and laughers if we are going to be effective leaders.

By loving, I obviously do not mean getting romantically involved with those whom we supervise or with those whom we serve. In fact, that is one of the great problems in our modern life. Instead, what I mean by loving is caring: nurturing, encouraging, and guiding those who work for us.

By laughter, I mean learning to bring genuine comedy into tense and complex situations. You say, "But I am just not the stand-up comic type." Then let others provide the comic relief. Far more importantly, if you want to help make brittle situations more pliable, look for humor in the dilemmas you face. And every situation has some element of comedy in it.

Love

Let me suggest seven specific ways that can help you beam genuine love into what may seem to be impossibly bad—even hate ridden—situations.

1. *Care for others.* Caring for people is an art that we need to learn for successful living. I remember one particular situation in which a teacher who had become legally blind continued to teach. Things were going from bad to worse with increased discipline problems, parents' complaints, and poor instruction for students. Action needed to be taken.

I decided to visit this teacher and counsel him to explore the possibility of going on disability. It was an option the teacher had never considered, and he was encouraged to inquire into this option. The disability was approved. He thanked me for caring, because he had not known what to do and he needed an income to support his family.

At some time, we all have to make difficult decisions that adversely affect others. When this happens, we must seek ways to help the ones affected. We should make known our concern and see that their dignity and human worth are maintained. I had just such an experience with an alcoholic teacher. His addiction was resulting in his poor performance. Though this problem had been obvious for quite some time, he had never been confronted about it. I discussed his problem with him, indicating my desire to help him. I assured him that our ultimate goal was to keep him as a teacher if he would secure proper treatment.

He agreed to take a leave of absence. He was finally placed in a situation that for the first time forced him to acknowledge he had a problem. This teacher later returned to the classroom after he was cured of his illness.

One year we had to lay off some forty-five teachers. It was a difficult but necessary decision since enrollment had dropped significantly over the past few years. I wrote a personal letter of reference for each teacher, and I made telephone calls to school districts that were increasing in enrollment in different parts of the United States. The situation was bad, but we were committed to try everything we could to make it good.

I have visited thousands of classrooms over the years and have noted the incredibly high correlation between a teacher's caring attitude and the students' enthusiasm for learning. I remember a particular visit to a third-grade classroom, taught by Miss Bonnie Hubbard. I was impressed with the warm and caring climate she had created, one that was reflected in the enthusiastic attitude of her pupils. After greeting the class, Miss Hubbard commented in her quiet and unassuming manner, "In this class we love a lot, we read a lot, and we learn a lot." (In 1983 Miss Hubbard was named Teacher of the Year by the local Sertoma Club; she passed away the next October.)

This school, though located in a somewhat lower socioeconomic section of the community, ranked surprisingly high in its overall achievement scores. The fourth-grade class has been "Mathematics Olympics" champion for all three years since the inception of the district-sponsored competition. As I became better acquainted with other teachers in Miss Hubbard's building, I found that most of them reflected a common philosophy of genuine caring for their students and a joy in their teaching.

Our caring must be more than attitude. Caring is ultimately action.

2. *Reinforce others' strengths.* Delegate tasks to people you know will succeed. This action will encourage the

individuals to strive for excellence.

Many times an organization fails because people are placed in situations where they make limited contributions. People want to do things at which they are best. If given the opportunities to show their talents in the areas of their strengths and interests, they will produce positive results.

That is true for a family, too. If the diversified talents of its members are appropriately pooled and used, family ties will be strengthened. Assigning responsibility in the area of individuals' strengths is a wise investment in their success. It also lets them know that you love and care for them.

3. *Use nonverbal communication.* The power of a touch, a hug, and a smile is limitless. The opportunities I have had for such direct interaction with students continuously reaffirms this. I experience their sensitivity, sincerity, and caring and loving attitudes.

One of the easiest and most effective ways to communicate our love is through the medium of a smile. We can uplift one another with a smile and a friendly touch of encouragement. If people in a community, a school, or an organization make a common pledge to greet every person with a smile, that organization will begin to radiate love.

An eighty-five-year-old man without friends and relatives to call on him was visited in the local hospital by a seminary student who was training to become a hospital chaplain. As soon as this student walked into the room, the old man's eyes filled with tears, and he asked, "Would you hug me?" The young man readily did so, but he was visibly shaken by the emotional impact of the incident.

Yearning to be loved is present in every heart. How many of our elderly people are living in this loneliness, needing a touch, a friendly smile, love! We need to reach out to people of all ages in all walks of life in a spirit of love and caring.

4. *Maintain your accessibility and availability.* A few years ago, a teacher walked into the administrative offices at about 5:30 P.M. I happened to be the only one in the office. She was obviously upset. When she saw me, she asked, "Is there someone around I can talk to?"

"Everyone is gone," I replied. "But if you wish, you may talk with me." She came into my office and shared her frustration with me for over an hour. When she left, she seemed to feel better. A few days later I got a note from her expressing appreciation for my accessibility at a time when she desperately needed someone to listen to her.

Since my job involves managing people, I choose to spend 30 to 40 percent of my time visiting the ones I manage. My purpose is not to evaluate performance as such, but to establish an atmosphere that encourages direct interaction with both the young people and the teachers. To watch master teachers at work is exciting. Accessibility is crucial to avoid potential problems. I would far rather wear out the soles of my shoes than the seat of my slacks.

In order to discipline myself to give time to this personal interaction phase of my work, I have made the following rules for myself.

a. *Take charge of myself and my schedule.* Recognize that there is an unconscious and unplanned conspiracy to keep me occupied with paperwork and the mundane activities associated with administration.

b. *Clearly identify my priorities.* Manage my time rather than be managed by it. Make room for people. When under pressure, one's ability to respond to situations correspondingly diminishes, resulting in lost time and added stress. By being out in the school buildings, the shop, or wherever, I am able to become aware of concerns and take appropriate measures before they become major problems demanding drastic action.

c. *Be visible.* When my presence is familiar, I can better relate to workers, and in turn they can respond more comfortably to me. My visits with students and staff leave me feeling inspired and thus better able to tackle the more mundane aspects of my work. The positivity that has been radiated during my visits helps me to be more productive.

d. *Know my people.* They will, in turn, appreciate knowing me. Know the people with whom I work, and share in their lives. They will respond to that personal interest. One time a teacher who was getting a divorce stopped in to see me and share her feelings. The problem was not necessarily related to her work, but my availability somewhat helped her at a critical time.

5. *Express your feelings in words.* Young people need to hear the words *I love you, We love you,* or *We are proud of you.* This will help them develop a healthy attitude and make self-giving an active part of their lives.

Parents have often expressed to me their feelings of helplessness to counteract the power of negative peer influence in their children's lives. To them, I would ask, "Have you listened to the nonverbal messages your children have tried to communicate? Have you told them you love them? Have you affirmed them with words of praise?"

Words like *You're terrific* are heard less and less frequently as children grow older and enter their teen years. Young people hear the word *love* more often from their peers than from their parents. Thus they form their own "peer culture" (and drug culture) in order to gain acceptance and feel needed, wanted, and loved. Let us not underestimate the power words exert. A constant supportive communication between parents and their children can often offset peer problems.

The same, of course, is true in your workplace. One never knows when, by reaching out to others, we influence another's life for good. Our very words may make a positive difference in the life of some troubled person.

6. *Support persons in authority.* Being sensitive to individuals in authority can also enhance their self-confidence. Take time to send a note or express a word of appreciation to those who supervise you. In my world, the members of the board of education are often the subject of open criticism. Wouldn't it be wonderful if some citizen appeared before the board of education (or the city council or the county commission) and said, "I am here just to let you know how much my family and I appreciate your service. I consider it my duty to thank you."

These public servants handle many bad situations and make them good. Their dedication and service deserve to be recognized. Many boards serve without pay, desiring only to build better communities. Let your community leaders, your pastors, your supervisor on the job know that you appreciate him or her. If you are in a bad situation, you can often change your supervisor's attitude for the better by seeing that individual's good qualities and letting him or her know of your love and gratitude.

7. *Inspire persons around you.* Dedicated teachers inspire students by their love. Fortunate are the young people who have great teachers to inspire in them a sense of self-confidence, a desire to learn, a concern for others, and an awareness of what they can be.

I have encountered many teachers who are motivated by love and are able to create loving schools where students concentrate not only on what they learn but also on how they live. With love and a touch of patience and perseverance, these teachers are able to make schools inviting places with a healthful learning climate to shape the lives of their students.

Our schools must become places where pupils, as soon as they walk into the room, receive a verbal and/or nonverbal message, "We are glad you are here! Together we are going to have a great day. You are going to make my day a joyful day." This reflects a spirit of positive anticipation. These teachers have not lost their zest of living. They do not lack a larger vision—a purpose.

Teachers with this loving attitude are able to help their students who lack self-confidence or self-esteem, or who have limiting thoughts. Their emphasis is on "I can" rather than "I.Q." They have high expectations of their pupils. They help students to discover the power of the positive "Three L's"—listen, love, and lend a hand—to counteract the negative "Three L's" of lack, loss, and limit. These teachers also apply the power of positive articulation to offer praise and words of encouragement to their students. Loving schools thus become effective schools where students are accepted as they are; they receive affections and are expected to achieve.

Laugh

The massive societal changes in recent decades have left our nation in a state of stress, frustration, and bewilderment. We are a nation in need of laughter.

The absence of love and laughter has meant an absence of proper coping mechanisms to deal with this stress. Physicians and psychologists are of the opinion that unresolved stress plays a major role in heart disease, high blood pressure, ulcers, and migraine headaches. By the simple act of learning to laugh properly, life can become a lot more pleasant.

I returned to my office one afternoon after my regular visits to several schools. I was on cloud nine. My spirits had been uplifted by being with the students and teachers.

I had just entered my office when two of my colleagues walked in. I could see by their faces that they were upset. Both of them, one after the other, had received calls from a father who was not only unreasonable and confrontational but also abusive in language. They told me, "You should have been here to talk to this guy."

I knew the situation needed comic relief. With a smile I answered, "Well, friends, when I get up in the morning, I pray, Lord, put me in the right place at the right time. You can see that He hears my prayers." There was hearty laughter. Soon we forgot about the morning phone complaints and looked at the possibilities of the afternoon.

While I was in graduate school at Bowling Green, I told my advisor about my expectation to become a superintendent of schools. I wanted to make sure that I took all the appropriate courses to be as well prepared as possible to compete successfully for a job. My advisor offered to discuss the matter with Superintendent Kaczenski under whom I had just completed my administrative internship.

After a week or so my professor called me in and said that John Kaczenski had a perfect suggestion to prepare me for a superintendency. You can well imagine my attentiveness and eager anticipation as he proceeded.

"Kaczenski suggests that if you change your name from Chopra to Chopraski and stay out of the sun, you will do all right." I laughed, knowing I had their confidence and support to continue with my goals. It was just the kind of response I needed.

My visits to the schools produce many amusing encounters. Keeping a healthy mental outlook is easy when you surround yourself with children. I recently visited a class of hearing-impaired children. A little nine-year-old boy sat watching me—actually, he was staring at me—with deep concentration. All of a sudden he burst out, with a touch of candor and sincerity, "Do you know you have a long nose?"

What could I do but laugh and answer, "You are right! My mother used to tell me that, too!" I always will remember the innocent look on the boy's face.

Another time I visited one of the kindergarten classrooms in Shawnee Mission. The teacher had prepared the class well for my coming. They knew my name with perfect pronunciation—Cho-pra—and had prepared a series of questions. As we were discussing the responsibilities of the superintendent of schools, one of the students asked, "How many hours a day do you work?"

As a new superintendent, I responded that I had been working about ten to twelve hours a day.

This young boy responded, "Dr. Chopra you ought to be laid off." There was a burst of laughter. I learned later that this youngster's dad had been laid off. The boy saw him around the house far more than he had before. He associated being laid off with having a good rest.

In the beginning of the school year, I was visiting a first-grade classroom. The teacher was in her forties and had an excellent, hard-earned tan from the summer months. She asked her class, "Do you know this gentleman?"

One boy, after some reluctance, raised his hand. "He is your son."

My exit from that classroom was an exceptionally

speedy one as I nearly collapsed in laughter in the hall. The teacher and I often chuckled over the boy's remark.

Dr. Viktor Frankl, whom I have mentioned previously, stated that while in the Gestapo prison camp, where atrocities and miseries imposed on humans by other humans went beyond imagination, humor provided them with the ability to cope. He wrote,

> Humor was another of the soul's weapons in the fight for self preservation. It is well known that humor, more than anything else in the human make up, can afford an aloofness and an ability to rise above any situation, even if only for a few seconds. I practically trained a friend of mine who worked next to me on the building site to develop a sense of humor.... The attempt to develop a sense of humor and to see things in a humorous light is some kind of a trick learned while mastering the art of living.[1]

In late 1980, a scheme to get rich through chain letters was revived and spread across the nation. It was considered by some, particularly the organizers of the plan, a fast way to get ahead monetarily without working.

Seizing upon the chain-letter idea an anonymous superintendent, recognizing the increasingly short tenure of school superintendents, wrote a letter addressed to all school board members throughout the nation.

Dear Board Members:

If you are unhappy with your superintendent, simply have your school board send a copy of this letter to six other schools who are tired of their superintendents.

Then bundle up your superintendent and send him to the school at the top of the list in the letter. Add the name of your school to the bottom of the letter.

Within a week, you will receive 16,435 superintendents

and one of them will be a dandy. Have faith in this chain letter for superintendents. Do not break the chain. One school broke the chain and got their old superintendent back!

> Sincerely yours,
>
> A Friendly Superintendent

A recent and well-publicized example of the power of laughter is the case of Norman Cousins, the former distinguished editor of *Saturday Review*. In 1964, Cousins was lying close to death in his hospital bed with collagen, a disease of the connective tissues. After he was told by his doctor that he had but a few months to live (in the opinion of a specialist his chance for recovering was one in five hundred), he immediately checked out of the hospital.

Cousins remembered reading books on stress written by Hans Selye, a pioneer in stress research. Selye outlined the effects of negative emotions on the chemistry of the human body. Cousins concluded that if negativity and stress could make him that sick, positivity and laughter could help him get well.

In consultation with his physician, Cousins initiated what he called full exercise of the affirmative emotions. He writes, "It was easy enough to hope and love and have faith, but what about laughter? It worked out I made the joyous discovery that ten minutes of genuine belly laughter had an anesthetic effect and would give me at least two hours of pain free sleep."[2]

Norman Cousins's miraculous recovery despite heavy odds and poor prognosis exemplifies the capacity of the human mind and body to regenerate. He read comic strips, watched the Marx brothers films and old "Candid Camera" TV shows sent by producer Allen Funt. Cousins is living proof of the power of laughter and its impact on an "incurable disease."

Once I visited a third-grade teacher in an elementary school. She told me she had been working long and hard to help a certain student improve his behavior and attitude. After a reading session that was continuously disrupted by this student, the teacher in her frustration said to the boy, "John, I am going to turn you over to God."

Another boy who happened to be walking by said, "Mrs. Jones, God is going to give him right back to you."

The laughter that followed this spontaneous comment helped the teacher begin to overcome her frustration. She decided to look at John as a boy who deserved and needed care. He began to respond, and today he is making steady progress. And what got this healing process going? A simple laugh.

Love and laughter are proven medicine for healing the heart, the mind, and the body. The Bible says, "Love suffers long and is kind; love...bears all things, believes all things, hopes all things, endures all things. Love never fails" (1 Cor. 13:4–8). The same is true of our sense of humor!

10

Pursue the Dream

Although I had signed a teaching contract in 1969 with the Toledo, Ohio, public schools at an annual salary of $8,600, I asked them to release me so I could accept a $4,000-a-year doctoral fellowship at Bowling Green State University. I chose the lesser pay, even though I knew that my pursuit of a terminal degree would require an initial sacrifice and demanding study.

After a particularly long day at the university, I was greeted by our five-year-old son, Dick, with the words, "Dad, why can't we live in a better house? Why did we come here? We had a good house in New Delhi."

It is sometimes difficult to explain such things to a five-year-old child. I told him I did not yet have a good enough job to afford a better house.

His immediate question was, "Why don't you get a good job?"

For some unknown reason, I said, "I do not know President Hollis Moore well enough to ask him." (Dr. Moore was the president of the university.) It was the end of the conversation as far as I was concerned.

The next day Dick happened to have a day off from

school, and he asked my sister, Santosh, who was staying with us while attending the university, to take him to President Moore. My sister, not realizing what was going on in young Dick's mind, agreed to take him. She thought that after visiting the campus and having an ice-cream cone, Dick would be satisfied to return home. Not so. With Santosh in tow, Dick got on the elevator to go to the eighth floor of the administration building.

As soon as they got out of the elevator and before she could persuade him to go back home, Dick left her hand and quickly approached a receptionist. He asked if he could see President Moore. Dr. Moore, who happened to be standing nearby, was somewhat intrigued by this five-year-old visitor. He took him into his office, leaving my embarrassed sister in the hallway. After five minutes, Dick emerged from the office with a victorious smile.

As soon as I walked into the house that evening, Dick enthusiastically said, "Dad, I did it for you!" Sue and my sister told me the whole episode. I received a letter a short while later from the president's office inquiring about my job situation. I also received a summons from the dean's office. But while everyone understood, it was awkward to explain the desire of a five-year-old boy who wanted his dream of living in a better house fulfilled earlier than my progress would warrant.

The house we were living in had a small living room and two very small bedrooms. We hung our clothes on a steel rod over our bed. Heating was provided by old, open-flame gas heaters, and we covered our doors and windows with plastic to help keep us warm as well as to save on energy bills.

While driving with a friend through a neighborhood in downtown Detroit in 1970, I commented how big and nice the houses were. He stared at me with surprise and commented, "We are driving through the slums of Detroit." I realized that these houses, compared to the one we were living in, presented a better picture for me. Living in that small house never deterred us from envisioning what our eventual home would be like.

Excuse Me While I Brag Us Up!

Americans in the past two decades have been overcritical of themselves. They have heard for so long what is wrong with them that the quiet voices of what is right with America and the American people have either been muffled or ignored. As a result they have not been fully in tune with their sense of optimism and the helping spirit with which they are blessed. A continuing evaluative analysis may help us to develop and grow, but this analysis must also include things for which we are grateful and thus serve as a motivational force to make the bad good and the good better.

This is the best nation I know in which to make a bad situation good. Her people have been known for their commitment, dedication, and ability to overcome adversities as demonstrated from the very first day that 102 people stepped off a little ship in Plymouth, Massachusetts. Theirs was a special dream.

So is the dream today of the immigrants of many national origins and cultural backgrounds. That is why thousands of them become U.S. citizens every year. Americans have adopted millions of people from all over the world who came to this country with the hope of finding the freedom and justice they failed to realize in their homeland. There are others who come to share in the abundance and contribute to the continuing greatness of America.

What is good and beautiful in America is not alone manifested in its majestic mountain peaks, mighty rivers, wondrous forests, broad plains, serene lakes, and skyscrapers. The wonder of America does not merely include the fruit of California, the corn of Iowa, the wheat of Kansas, the oil of Texas, and the industries of Pennsylvania. The real wonder of America lies in the giving and helping spirit of its people. Thousands of first-generation immigrants can relate stories and experiences that reflect the caring and encouragement they have received from American people in realizing their dreams.

People really helped my family. I remember the generosity of the landlady who rented us her home in Bowling Green. Knowing that our worldly possessions consisted of only three suitcases, she gave us her fully furnished home, including pots and pans, dishes, sheets, blankets, and even towels. Mr. and Mrs. Feller, owners of a laundromat, drove Sue to the doctor's office for regular checkups during her pregnancy, since we had no car.

In October 1970, our only daughter, Komal, was born. Again our friends came to our aid. Mr. and Mrs. M. D. Beard who had adopted us earlier came to our assistance. Mrs. Beard drove about forty miles each way every day to take care of Dick and Lucky and prepare meals for us while Sue was in the hospital and I attended classes at the university.

David (a local dentist) and Shelly Harkness were always there to take our children for swimming lessons in the summer and to the ice arena for skating in the winter. Don Schlueter, a teacher, and his wife Norma, a nurse in the local hospital, introduced us to farm life. Their parents were farmers, and through them we came to know of the industry, hospitality, and determination of the American farmer.

During my graduate studies I served as an intern under John Kaczenski, superintendent of the Lakota schools. He gave me my first administrative break by appointing me principal of the Bradner School.

With the help of many people, I was getting closer to my goal. John Kaczenski had played a very important role in my growth. His leadership and kindness tremendously encouraged me.

The greatness of America continued to manifest itself through the supporting and encouraging actions of my fellow graduate students and professors in the College of Education at Bowling Green State University. I discovered that the professors not only possessed great minds but also were blessed with caring hearts.

The beauty of America was revealed to us through the friendly and giving attitude of the citizens in Bowling Green, Bradner, Sandusky, Medina, and Bellefontaine, all in Ohio. Our lives continued to be enriched by the loving and caring spirit of citizens in Council Bluffs, Iowa, and Shawnee Mission, Kansas. We saw the great American spirit reaching out and enfolding us again and again.

Dream Big Dreams

In late June 1976, I received a call from Bellefontaine, Ohio, inviting me to come for a personal interview concerning the school superintendency there. You can imagine our excitement, joy, and enthusiasm for this first interview opportunity after submitting over two hundred applications.

I reached the board of education offices at 8:00 P.M., ready for the interview scheduled for 8:15. As I opened the door, Bill Troop, president of the board, greeted me and said that they would call me in soon. Since there was no waiting room, I walked out to the parking area and strolled to a beautiful spot at its edge, surrounded by tall trees. I looked up toward the late June sky, full of blinking stars hanging like diamonds. As I gazed upward I thought about my dream and how close I had come in such a short time.

Then, as I waited, doubting thoughts began to penetrate my mind: "The board members have worked hard all day and are tired. They are already interviewing a candidate, and when my turn comes, they will probably be weary and not in the best of spirits." I flushed the negative thoughts from my mind and replaced them with positive thoughts: "Those board members are concerned about their young people and recognize the single most important function the board ever discharges is the selection of a superintendent."

I walked back and forth refurbishing my mind with success thoughts. It reminded me of a walk I took in the 110-degree heat in New Delhi while I was searching for a job. I recalled how miraculously things had changed for me then. I became convinced that positive forces were once again working in my life. I prayed, "Dear God, help me. What I am is Your gift to me and what I become is offered as my gift to You." My spirits soared, and I grew increasingly enthusiastic about this one interview opportunity.

I was called in at about 9:00 P.M., forty-five minutes behind schedule. It was not an encouraging situation. I was introduced to three very kind and gracious ladies, Mrs. Joan Kelly, Mrs. Marilyn Miller, and Mrs. Olga Henry. The other two board members, Mr. Dean Hess and Mr. William Troop, were also friendly and warm. The interview that I was previously told would last about an hour concluded at 12:30 A.M.—three and one-half hours long! I must say I was impressed with both the quality of the questions and the positive attitude of the board members, and I felt reasonably good about my performance.

I had no sooner reached my motel room than the telephone rang. It was Mr. Troop expressing the board's desire to have breakfast the next morning with my family. I readily and happily agreed. Sue, who almost always sleeps well, was unable to sleep that whole night. She prayed with a sense of positive anticipation. I, too, was full of faith and hope.

After breakfast, which was just a friendly, get-acquainted time, we returned to Medina. In the next few days, members of the board from Bellefontaine visited Medina, and some of them even went to Sandusky to check on references there in the community. The job was offered to me that same evening. There was a special air of thanksgiving and gratitude in our home. Our faith in the American people had once more been confirmed. While I had applied for over two hundred positions, I needed only one job offer. As far as I was concerned, that would mean I was 100 percent successful.

During one of our house-hunting visits prior to taking over my new duties in Bellefontaine, my family and I were having dinner in a local restaurant. A gentleman who recognized me from pictures he had seen in the local newspaper came to our table. "Are you the new superintendent?" he asked. I responded affirmatively. He congratulated me, and we talked together for a few minutes. As he was about to leave, he placed a buckeye in my hand and said, "You are in the wonderful buckeye state. This is for good luck. God will help you." We were touched by this man's warm spirit. My wife still carries the buckeye with her, and so far, it has given us all the man promised.

Instead of criticizing the country, we need to use our energy to help those in need of help. We need to ask ourselves, "Are we working in our jobs to the fullest extent?" One needs to look himself or herself in the eye in a mirror and pose the questions, "Am I holding back on my job? Am I trying to get by and give only the minimum? Is my work ethic as strong as that of previous generations? Am I enjoying the results of the sweat and blood of my ancestors without adding my contribution to ensure the continuing greatness of America?"

There is still lots of room for people to work hard to succeed—far more so than anywhere else in the world. On an everyday basis the helpful American people are making many bad situations good for individuals and families throughout this great nation.

Citizenship By Choice

Another highlight in my realizing the American dream came in March 1976, the bicentennial year, when I chose to become a United States citizen. It was a thrilling moment in my life. Sue chose to wait until our two sons, Dick and Lucky, were mature enough to decide for themselves. In December 1982, she and Lucky were naturalized, and Dick followed in February 1983. Both boys fully recognize their new responsibilities as citizens. My older son, Dick, after taking the oath remarked, "I can hardly wait to vote." I say with a great deal of pride, "I am an American by choice."

This wonderful experience of becoming a citizen was relived when in March 1984 I was invited by a federal judge to speak before more than sixty people from more than twenty-seven different countries who were being sworn in as new U.S. citizens. Their excitement and enthusiasm can be appreciated to the fullest extent only by those who have experienced life in other places. After the ceremony, I talked with these new citizens. They considered U.S. citizenship a privilege and honor. They knew what freedom in the United States meant to them.

In my speech to the group, I challenged them to carry

a flaming torch of love and to tell every natural born American citizen they meet how wonderful he or she is. We as first-generation immigrants must tell Americans about their kindness and helping hands. Every newly naturalized citizen ought to express his or her appreciation for the goodness of the American people by looking them straight in the eye and saying, "You are wonderful. You are beautiful. You are generous. You are special."

We may never be able to pay back what we have received, but we can play an important role by uplifting the spirit of our fellow citizens. This is a noble opportunity to accentuate the good. We chose to become citizens. It is always a privilege to have a choice, but with choice also comes the responsibility to be responsible, contributing citizens.

Taking Freedom for Granted

We take our liberty and abundance of freedom for granted. In December 1982, while on a speaking engagement at Bowling Green, Ohio, I had the opportunity to visit with a professor whom I had known for many years. As I was sharing with him my positive attitude toward America, he related to me an experience he had during a recent visit to East Germany from where he had originally emigrated.

After spending a week in West Germany and getting all his travel documents in order, he crossed the border into East Germany to visit his relatives. Through a mix-up in communication, he found that they were in a different town. But when he wanted to transfer there, the East German authorities would let him go only to the place for which his visa was approved. They refused to change the name of the town on the visa. He said, "I realized as never before what our freedom in the U.S.A. means."

In the summer of 1983, I had the opportunity to visit with a well-educated man who with his wife and two children had escaped from Afghanistan. "My family and I traveled in the high mountains over rough terrain during the night and hid in the caves during the day in order to escape to Pakistan," he told me. "We were not sure whether we would make it or not, but we chose to risk our lives to escape the horrors of Soviet domination." He continued, "The Soviet Union is systematically destroying the fiber of the society by eliminating the intelligentsia and closing schools and colleges. The best way to rule people is to keep them ignorant by depriving them of educational stimulation, which encourages one to think, analyze, and question."

This man, though a graduate of Ohio State University with a degree in broadcasting, had to spend one year in Afghan refugee camps in Pakistan. He described the deplorable conditions there. After one year of struggle, he reached the United States. Even though at the time of our visit he was without a job, he considered himself blessed to be able to breathe the air of freedom. "My family is surviving with the help of generous American people and community churches," he said.

Our Legacy of Dreamers

Americans can look to their models, Ben Franklin, Thomas Edison, Henry Ford, Alexander Graham Bell, the Wright brothers, and many others who have exhibited American resolve and creativity. For example, when Japan stopped the rubber supply during World War II, we invented synthetics as a substitute, and a new manufacturing era was born. And no other nation has had as many Nobel Prize winners as the United States.

When others had failed and said the Panama Canal could never be built, the United States responded in typical fashion with a yes, we can. American scientists developed the aerospace technology that put the first man on the moon. American engineers developed the microchip, which has opened up the sophisticated computerization that impacts the world's technology in thousands of ways.

Our forefathers with their will power, hard work, and imagination tackled the dangers of the wilderness to give us a beautiful land full of abundance. Other generations fought the Revolutionary War and the Civil War to unite us as a strong nation. Others made sacrifices during the Great Depression to hand over to us a legacy of prosperity.

How do we want to be remembered by the coming generations? What legacy do we want to pass on to our children? I would hope our answer would reflect the hard-working, pioneer spirit of our forefathers. Will we be remembered as a generation that stood the test of time and not only brought America to the twenty-first century with advancements in technology but also with a legacy of peace and prosperity?

Heaven Is Here

My mother visited us here in the States in 1979 for six months. As we were having dinner the night before her return to India, she said, "Ten years ago, when you announced one fine morning you had a dream and you would be leaving India for good, I was angry and upset. I could not understand why you would leave your brother and sisters, your relatives and friends, and your promising career to pursue an unknown and unsure dream with only a few dollars in your pocket. I was so disturbed that I could not forgive you."

As I listened, I carefully watched her expression.

"Today," she continued, "I am forgiving you. Now I

understand what you mean by the American dream." In the next phrase she made a most important statement, "It is heaven here." My mother was in a position to know, for she has traveled in many countries with my brother, Inder Vir.

Americans should feel no self-imposed guilt. They are among the world's most giving, caring, and sharing people. Heaven is a paradise we anticipate, but we are living in a heaven of sorts here where we can dream dreams and where people reach out to help each other make those dreams a reality. You, America, made my dream a reality. You are wonderful, you are generous, and you are caring.

As I complete this chapter during Thanksgiving week, I feel all of us need to extend the spirit of this season to every day for the rest of our lives for the blessings of liberty and abundance we enjoy in this great nation. This spirit of thanksgiving will not permit us to take everything we have for granted but inspire us to rededicate ourselves to the principles, vision, and faith with which the pilgrims entered this virgin land.

The great American dream—is it alive and well, or a flash from the past? It is alive and well, fellow Americans. And dreams just like my own are coming true every day in this nation. The reality of those dreams should be measured not only by how much money you earn but also by how well you have given of yourself. And if you will keep dreaming the dream, you will be amazed to find how your gratefulness for this country will carry you through the bad situations and help turn them to good.

To believe, to look for the good, to be enthusiastic and expect the best, to dare to make a difference, to love and laugh, and to dream the American dream—this is the essence of positive living. America, you are great because your people are good.

Part III

The Practicalities

11

Making a Good Marriage Better

Technically, I suppose, one could argue that a chapter on marriage might be "out of sync" with the rest of this book. But there are so many bad situations in the homes of otherwise decent families that I was impressed to say a particular word to this most sensitive area of life.

Recently, during one of my visits to an elementary school, I had lunch with a group of first graders. In the course of our conversation, a little girl sitting next to me expressed her excitement over a square dance program to be held at her school that evening. She was looking forward to participating in it. I asked if her mom and dad would be accompanying her. She responded that her mom would come but that her dad did not live with them.

Another student, struggling with his spaghetti, piped up that his dad made better spaghetti; I learned he cooked it almost every day for this young boy and his third-grade sister. "My mom does not live with us," he explained.

I feel deeply for these young people. Against this

single-parent backdrop, I have come to a new realization of the increasing role of the school as a *family* of people working together. Why? This burgeoning phenomena of the single-parent family is placing new demands on society in general, and on the school systems in particular, all across the nation. But besides addressing that problem, what can we do to stop the growing epidemic of broken homes?

A Lasting Arrangement

I have been blessed with the love and support of my wife, Sukant (our friends in the United States call her "Sue"). In her I have found a life partner who is a paragon of virtue. Our relationship supports the old cliché that marriages are made in heaven. Though heaven certainly had a part in it, our marriage was arranged by our parents. Arranged? Of course!

To most people in the Western world, the idea of an arranged marriage may seem preposterous. When I mention how Sue and I were selected for one another by our parents, high school students and older adults commonly ask, "How can you love a spouse without having the freedom of personal selection?" or "How does an arranged marriage work?"

The answer to these questions may be as intriguing as the idea of arranged marriage itself. In the Western world you first fall in love, and then you make the commitment to marry. This sequence is reversed in an arranged marriage. You first make a lifelong commitment to each other; then you fall in love.

But if we can move beyond the basic premise of "choice" versus "arranged" for a moment, a better understanding of the concept can be developed.

In my case, one day after I returned home from work,

my mother proudly announced that she had visited with a girl's family to arrange for our marriage. Her words did not startle me since I had heard such announcements regarding other marriage arrangements all my life. It was, however, a bit arresting to hear the pronouncement of *my* marriage.

Being an educated person with a college degree, I was, however, given the privilege of having a look at my prospective wife before the marriage—if I so desired. In cases of young men and women from rural areas or less educated families, the parents may make the decision about a marriage arrangement without any involvement of the future bride and bridegroom. I accepted my mother's invitation without a second thought. I knew that any delay in responding would be quickly interpreted by my mother as acquiescence to her decision.

The time was set for our visit to the home of my prospective bride. Arriving there on the scheduled day, we settled in the living room, and the traditional tea was served to extend the family's hospitality to us. Soon after we arrived, a shy young lady with lovely dark eyes and long black hair walked into the room and sat across from me.

Decision time was suddenly here! We all talked informally. My mother, grandmother, sisters, and brother all seemed quite happy with the girl. The parents of the young lady voiced their approval of me, and my mother in turn communicated her approval of Sue. So we all lifted our teacups for a final sip, and the arrangement was underway. Of course, I concurred with the family decision. Did I have any fear? Yes, the fear of the unknown—which most Westerners, by the way, have as well!

Before my mother had suggested the girl to me, she had done her own "compatibility study." That is, Sue's family background and her family's status in the community, her height, her educational background, and other such factors were all taken into account. Sue's parents also undertook a similar checkup on me, including a prognostication into my future economic potential. The final decision in our case—as with most Indian couples—was thus reached on the basis of intellect, not simply emotions.

Sue and I remained engaged for ten months before our wedding. During this time, neither of us made any effort to contact the other. There was suspense as well as anticipation. There was fear, but an even greater degree of hope and trust.

The most embarrassing moment of the arranged marriage comes after the wedding, when the couple is alone together for the first time. In our case, we took the whole first day to get to know each other. We looked together at our future from a realistic viewpoint. Then, we began to express the intimacy of our new love—a love that continues to grow each day. We were married first; then we began to fall in love in all its fullness.

Why do I rehearse all this? Do I believe everyone ought to have our experience of living life with a marriage partner selected by someone else? No. Instead I unveil our arranged-for vows because we are talking about making a good marriage better—or perhaps making a bad marriage good. And odd as it may sound, marriages in trouble may not make the grade merely by going back to feelings of romance. Most failing marriages had that element at their outset.

I tell our story to encourage you to renew your *commitment* to your spouse, a commitment without condition. Then, out of that commitment, work to build romance.

Or let me put it another way. In a very real sense, all

marriages are arranged marriages. First of all, God arranged your marriage. It was He who superintended the union in the first place. You say, "Well, what if we got married outside His will, in disobedience to Him?" Then at the very least, He allowed it. And the permissive will of God is always stronger than the directive will of man.

Then, too, you arranged your marriage. You entered into the relationship in full agreement. "But," you say, "I think I made a mistake."

Do you know that virtually everyone wonders about that at various stages in married life? It is such a subtle thing. The moment something goes wrong, we tend to rethink the whole relationship. "Maybe we weren't in love in the first place" is an excuse that is often put forth when two people contemplate divorce. Again, why do I bring this up? Because I am the guy, along with teachers and principals, who has to deal with the heartbroken, leftover kids.

Let me ask you a question. If your marriage is in trouble at this juncture of your life, would you be willing to confess it as being arranged? Maybe all you have to work with here is something very minimal: that God allowed you two to make a mistake to which you both agreed. Even if that is the best you can think of your marriage, remember that God loves you and that He could have stopped it if He had so chosen. And since He permitted the marriage, that says to me that it is far more "arranged" than you have given it credit for being.

"But," you say, "you don't know what I'm caught with. We are really struggling. I deserve something better."

I understand those first two statements. But I do not accept the third. The fact is, none of us deserves a thing. Everything we are and have has been given to us by God in His mercy. I think all of us have married out of our class. And when we are humble before the Lord, we have to say, "Lord, with all our bad days, this person you joined me to is still worthwhile, is still the one you arranged for me to love, and is still better than I deserve—even on my good days."

May I offer a suggestion? Tonight after work, when you return home, take your spouse aside where the two of you can be alone. Depending upon your individual circumstances and what is appropriate in your situation, say something like this: "Honey, tonight I'd like to recommit myself to you for the rest of my life. I know things have not gone like we thought they would. In saying this, I am not asking that you change in the areas we don't agree on and I am not promising that I will be everything you want me to be, though I am promising to try. But what I do believe is this, that God arranged our marriage to each other. So I am recommiting myself to you for the rest of our lives, no matter what, and I'm asking you to accept that recommitment."

In an arranged marriage, though those words may never be voiced, they are nonetheless the foundational attitude of the agreement. Arranged marriages do not stay together because the couple is always dreamy eyed over each other, constantly enthralled with each other's presence, consistently taken with warm, fuzzy feelings of romance and erotic attraction. Those categories belong to postmodern movie plots and TV soaps anyway! No, the thing that holds healthy marriages together is that the partners have that sense of being chosen, not of choosing. This creates an attitude of adaptability to each other with a renewed spirit and initiative for living and loving.

In this age of choice, let us always start by bowing to God's choice, not our own. Make His selections yours; validate His arrangements by the giving of your will.

Build on your union, which has already been set forever in place.

Someone recently asked Sue how she knew that her marriage would work. How could she have confidence in an arranged relationship with so little personal input from herself? Her answer was simple and straightforward: "I trusted my parents' wisdom and judgment beyond my own. I knew they would choose a far better mate for me than I would ever select for myself."

The arranged marriage removes the direct pressure from young men and women to make a lifetime choice and places the pressure on the parents. But beyond that, it makes the basis of the marriage a commitment between two families—a covenant, if you will—not merely the warm feeling of a lovely romance, feelings that will almost certainly fluctuate over the years ahead.

The One-Plus-One Theory

As I grew up, my grandmother, the great storyteller, strongly emphasized the importance of the family and regularly reinforced this idea in her quickwitted, inspirational way.

I remember her asking me one day, "What is one and one?"

As a proud eighth grader, I was not much impressed with Grandma's quiz. Grandmother, persistent as always, calmly and firmly demanded the answer. Finally, with some annoyance, I responded with the answer, "Two."

Again she asked, "What is one and one?"

I thought for a moment and simply stated, "Two."

She responded, "My son, one *plus* one is two, but one and one is eleven [11]."

She continued her story without giving me the opportunity to protest. "When a man marries a woman and starts a family, they have the strength and vitality of eleven people, even though mathematically they are two. Their selfless love for each other and their spiritual unity give these two people advantages equal to eleven people. They have become a team. With the birth of children in the family, new strength and more talents are added. Their enthusiasm for each other provides the power and push we all need to realize our dreams."

I have found an interesting parallel to this philosophy in the arranged relationships in which we have little choice out in the business world. As a superintendent in three different school districts, I learned to accept the fact that the employees—in particular the top executives—were already in place when I joined each district. I did not bring anyone with me to the new assignment. I had no choice except to do my best to make those arranged relationships work. The success of the school district depended on the success of those relationships. And at times, rough edges had to be smoothed and adjustments made to ensure the effective operation of the organization. Relationships in a family, as in any organization, require constant care, nurture, and communication as well.

All in the Family

My responsibility as superintendent of schools places heavy demands on my time, and I am under continous pressures. I have had to learn to improve the quality of time I spend with my family in order to overcome the lack of quantity.

Every Saturday morning our three children join my wife and me on our bed, and we have a good rap session for an hour or so. Sue and I listen to their successes and frustrations of the week. We provide sympathetic understanding to help heal feelings of perceived injustices they have suffered. But more importantly we take this opportunity to praise their achievements, challenge them, and express appreciation for their responsible attitudes. We talk about the excitement of the coming weeks. I also am able to share the highlights of my own week and my anticipation for the future. I sometimes tell them of humorous incidents that have taken place during my visits to various classrooms.

This Saturday morning family circle has become quite important for us. Once that basic commitment to each other is secured—or resecured—there are certain things we can do to *build* our relationships and make them better.

How can we strive to achieve the kind of success in our family relationships that we have in our business or vocation? What can busy people do to promote the care and maintenance of their families? Here are six suggestions that keep this arranged marriage perking:

1. *Communicate with your spouse.* It is important that husband and wife understand each other. They must have *common* goals and priorities—do not be successful alone, ever.

I happened to talk with a highly successful businessman who went through a heartbreaking experience of divorce. He admitted that he spent ten to twelve hours a day planning for success in his business. He invested time and money developing new products and researching new marketing techniques. "I succeeded in business," he said with a sigh, "but I failed in my family relations because I did not think of making a similar commitment and devotion of time and energy in planning for success in my marriage."

Sue and I came to the United States in September

1969, with full knowledge of the challenges and difficulties that lay ahead. Sue's unwavering love and support made the trials endurable. During our years of struggle, when I was working on my graduate degree, we had a common goal of succeeding or failing *together*. We had talked it over. The variable was not our marriage; it was how well I would do in school. Our love was here to stay.

Thus, the journey with this spirit of togetherness became easier and far less worrisome. If one of us felt low, the other served as uplifter to reinforce hope, optimism, and confidence for the future. But to accomplish this, we have had to communicate.

2. *Allow your children to participate in major decisions.* All our moves prior to coming to Shawnee Mission had been at a stage when our children were too young to think much of the move. But when I heard about the superintendent position opening up at the Shawnee Mission School District, I immediately shared it with the entire family. We sat together and talked about the move, the challenging educational opportunities for my own children as students, the emphasis on excellence in the district, and the overall quality of life in the new community.

That discussion led to a joint family decision: I ought to submit my letter of application. As I received additional material from Shawnee Mission School District, I encouraged my family to look over the literature. My purpose was to fan the spark of support I already had from my family into a flame of enthusiasm for the move when, and if, it happened.

When I received the phone call for a personal interview, the children got involved in preparing my credentials. My detailed resume submitted for the initial interview clearly reflects the talent of the whole family.

The compiling of information in seven separate sets, one for each board member, requires a great deal of time and effort.

My family thus assumed full responsibility for getting this data prepared and in the mail while I devoted my time to studying the historical background of the district over the past five years. My wife and children made helpful suggestions about improving the quality of information we put together to present a clear picture to the board of education of my abilities and commitment.

After the personal interview, Sue and the children looked forward to the next step. The board members' visit to our community for on-site reference checks brought my family's enthusiasm to a boiling point. They were involved. We had a common interest, a common stake, a common vision, and a common enthusiasm for the move—and they knew that!

Sue had an interesting experience after I had accepted the Shawnee Mission job. She ran into the wife of a local businessman who was moving on to a higher level position. She asked Sue if our son, who at the time was in the ninth grade, expressed his unhappiness and unwillingness to move from Council Bluffs.

Sue said, "No. As a matter of fact our children are excited about this new opportunity, even though our older son has to stay in Council Bluffs for a semester to complete his graduation requirements."

This lady indicated the unhappiness and unwillingness of her ninth-grade son in regard to their impending move. He did not want to be separated from his friends. But he had never been involved in the decision to move in the first place.

Our children were asked by a newspaper reporter, "Will you miss your friends?" And they responded, "Yes, but we will make new friends."

Bringing our families along in decision making can enhance the probability of accomplishing our goals. We can also strengthen our family relationships and move ahead together, with joyful anticipation, to a new challenge. When the commitment of the whole family is solid, a general sense of positive anticipation prevails.

3. *Verbalize and visibly express your love.* After we took our son to the university to begin his freshman year, I shook his hand and said, "Give it your best."

Sue looked at me with surprise and asked, "Aren't you going to hug him?"

I had not wanted to embarrass my eighteen-year-old in the presence of the other students who were standing around in the dormitory lobby. But when Sue objected, it dawned on me that I had been overtaken by the environment. I took a step toward Dick and hugged and kissed him. Dick was expecting this, and he hugged me in the same manner he had always done. "Dad, I love you," he said. He was not embarrassed by his surroundings; he was proud of this visible expression of my love. For us, it is normal to express our feelings for each other.

At times, we tend to be too sensitive to our environment. We forget that our example may encourage others to believe that outward expressions of love strengthen the fibers that tie a family together.

The pastor of a local church told me that many of the teen-agers he talks with say their parents never tell them they are loved. These young people are left to assume it, but like every one of us, they want, and need to *hear* it.

A recent letter written to "Dear Abby" by a twelve-year-old boy stated how he was continously nagged by his mother for not doing this thing or that right. She never told him she loved him. "I don't remember the last time she hugged me or paid me a compliment," he wrote.

We must have high expectations of our children, but

these expectations should not preclude compliments and recognition for the many noble and fine things our children do. We need to work to let our children know that we notice their good qualities.

4. *Schedule time together.* Just as you schedule business and civic appointments, schedule time for your family—and make these times inviolate.

When we were moving from Council Bluffs in 1982, my schedule was packed full with many official and social commitments. My secretary placed on my schedule a dinner with the members of the board of education for the day of our daughter's birthday. This was a disappointment for all of us, but it was too late for me to decline to attend.

From this experience my daughter learned something that taught me an excellent lesson. To my surprise, the next year Komal called my secretary two months prior to her birthday and asked that the evening be scheduled for her! I discovered her action a few days before her birthday when I saw my weekly schedule. Her placement on my schedule insured my availability to her that evening. Now Sue makes sure she is on the schedule for important occasions.

In Council Bluffs we reserved Wednesday evening as family night. All my school-sponsored activities would cease every Wednesday evening by 6:30 P.M. Only matters of extreme urgency ever intruded into this scheduled time with my family.

5. *Encourage one another in success or failure.* In a family each member in his or her own way provides a sympathetic ear. Everyone becomes a channel of communication, a voice of appreciation, a source of assistance and support in times of failure, someone to laugh with and to love in times of joy and sorrow. Family members serve in a variety of roles, such as coun-

selor, leader, friend, comforter, and motivator.

After a speech I gave recently, a man came up to me and explained that he was under excessive stress on his job because of his superior's complete lack of concern for him. He said, "Not only do I suffer distress while at the office, but I am shown no understanding, concern, and love when I get home."

My advice to him was this: "Unless you initiate love and kindness at home, you won't get much in return." His need was to get busy and set the pace.

A loving and caring family provides its members with strength, vitality, and encouragement. They overcome obstacles and make the hurdles of life new opportunities. Their support for each other inspires every member to attempt higher goals and loftier achievements.

6. *Forgive but never forsake.* We must be forgiving to strengthen our bonds with each other. In making a bad situation good, we must realize that to succeed in the world and fail at home is really not success.

Sue and I were talking with the wife of a very successful professional person concerning the importance of consistently communicating our love to our children. This woman confided that her daughter, now an adult, "did not know her father." The husband was so busy helping others, pursuing success in his career and achieving status in the community, that he missed the wonderful opportunity of sharing in the growing experiences of his daughter. This woman now has a son who has chosen the same career as his father, and she intends to point out to him the importance of loving, enjoying, and communicating with his family.

Not long ago the newspaper carried a story about an apparently emotionally disturbed junior high student who went to school with a loaded gun and began shooting. One student was fatally wounded. Imagine the remorse of the father whose son was dead. "We said a simple good-bye before my son left for school (Thursday) morning. As far as I am concerned, that just wasn't enough," he sobbed.

Those of us who still have the opportunity should not take this father's remorse lightly. Let us express our love to our children and to other human beings in positive ways. We can extend our love with a warm smile and say to every person we meet, "You are wonderful."

Once while Sue and I were traveling, she suddenly said, "I consider my purpose in life to give you joy and have joy with you." What a beautiful expression! All of us have responsibility to give joy to our spouses and to our loved ones.

What about those of you who truly have worked to improve your marriage, and yet your spouse has abandoned the commitment to you necessary for a healthy marriage? My word to you is this: pray for discernment and seek counsel. Do not give up easily as so many do today. However, some situations, especially where physical or mental abuse is present, must be abandoned.

The point is, do not settle for mediocrity in your marriage. Start today with a resolve to improve your relationships with your spouse and children, no matter what the past has held. Can you make a bad marriage good, or a good one better? Ninety-five percent of the time, yes! Do not believe the deception that would tell you otherwise.

12

Go for It!

You like me, no doubt, have learned that we can do little to control circumstances. In my work things happen, situations arise, and people make their moves—and then I find out about them! We cannot always prohibit bad situations from occurring; we can seek to turn them to good.

The thrust of this book, therefore, has not been to tell you how to make your circumstances better. Most of the time, to repeat, we have no control over the situations we face. But we do control one thing: the manner and attitude with which we react and respond to situations. The real difference, then, between positive and negative people, lies not in the circumstances themselves but in the way we face them.

We all face tragedies, such as death in the family, a dear one suffering from a terminal disease, or the loss of a limb in an accident. Sometimes these circumstances create questions in our minds about God's purpose. But it is when we can't understand the reason for these heartaches that we need more than ever to let God surround us. He will make us strong and help us to see the fulfillment of His purpose in the midst of the adverse situation.

But we must also remember that problems may not only stem from tragedies but also from triumphs. Dreamers and strivers who have experienced a measure of success early may later encounter huge problems that they will need to tackle.

The good news is, it's never too late for anyone to change! I read recently about a teen-ager who had become addicted to hard drugs. Use of these drugs would send him into a rage, to the point that he would consistently hurt others. Finally, one day he turned on himself. In a drug-induced stupor, he placed the barrel of a gun into his own mouth and pulled the trigger. Though this attempt to put an end to his life failed, it did result in the severing of his optic nerve. He survived, but he was left permanently blind.

This self-imposed suffering could hardly be thought of as the fulfillment of any purpose. What course could he take? Happily, he came to terms with his folly, and now this young man speaks to as many youth groups as he can to tell his peers that drug use produces dreadful results. He is committed to helping others avoid the same fate he suffered. This he considers his purpose in life.

Suffering? Adverse circumstances? We can't usually keep them from happening, but we can determine how we handle them. Realistic thinkers do not deny the existence of these adversities but look at them from a positive perspective. They seek for the pluses and make the most of them. In the midst of trials they search for their own purpose and relate the circumstances to that.

A young woman in Russia was arrested for teaching in a Bible school and was sentenced to a distant prison camp. The deplorable conditions there so affected her health that within a short period of time she looked much older than her actual age. When her mother visited her some years later, she was shocked at her condition. But despite the deplorable conditions in this prison camp, she said to her mother, "It is O.K. I have been able to spread the Word of God among over two thousand other women prisoners here who had never before heard the message of Jesus Christ. I am fulfilling a purpose."

What are your circumstances? Work to train yourself to respond to trials and turmoils with faith, not fear or self-pity. Consider the psalmist's words, "The steps of a good man are ordered by the LORD, / and He delights in his way. / Though he fall, he shall not be utterly cast down; / For the LORD upholds him with His hand" (Ps. 37:23–24).

I know of a student who was a competent drummer. But she was injured in an automobile accident and lost the thumb and index finger of her right hand. This physical disability placed severe limitations on her ability as a drummer. But she refused to accept the physical handicap and taught herself to set the rhythm with her left hand. By controlling her response and exercising a positive attitude, she is still working with her drum. I have full faith that she will be one of the best drummers our school district has ever had.

So with the story of another young student, Anna, who has been blind since birth. She has no control over her blindness, but she has a positive attitude about her problem. She graduated in 1984 in the top 1 percent of her class. She refused to accept any bondage from her limitation and responded with determination to excel.

Examples of young people like these are many. They love God and express their gratitude to Him by not giving in to their physical limitations. They believe in their purpose in life.

When you discover your life's purpose, you are better able to accept the reverses of life. The temptation to give up is minimized. Pursuing your purpose also brings you in touch with other people through whom God can work on your behalf. The feeling of being cared about and loved provides a kind of fertilization that nurtures your spirit and strengthens your resolve to be an overcomer.

Furthermore, a person whose life is blessed with giving and receiving love is a wholesome individual, one who is in tune both with his or her own self-worth and that of other people. Love is thus an all-important factor in developing a realistic perspective on life and controlling one's attitude and response to circumstances.

Whatever your station, you can still be in charge of your life. To set your course, you must have a vision, or dream, as well as a plan. Then you need to concentrate your efforts and act with faith to make the vision a reality.

It is a common tendency to waver when your vision is clouded and you cannot see the end of the road. You must be prepared to face the storms that threaten to obscure your view and to surmount the obstacles that inevitably stand in the way of your goals. No one can avoid obstacles. They must be met with courage and confidence. Failing is not the worst thing; not having tried is. Remember that despite the detractors, there are more people who want you to succeed than you realize.

Important though your goals and your commitment to accomplish them may be, they in themselves are not enough. You must supplement your efforts with realism—facing life as it is. You cannot afford to permit yourself to be taken down to the pit by your depressive emotions. Put your positive thoughts into action, and you will be better able to look for the good in the midst of the bad.

A few last comments are in order. The reason I like the term *realistic thinking* as a key to making bad situations good is this: not everyone is going to succeed to the same degree. Success is being realistic, not winning at any cost. Being average on the job in comparison with others, for example, must not be construed as being average in life. Your job is to give it your best shot and to keep shooting.

Reality thinking focuses on facing a problem or bad situation from a realistic, rational perspective, outlining alternatives and options, and choosing the best plan of action. Also, to succeed, we must be in command of our attitude. First and foremost, then, reality thinkers respond to a bad situation with a calculated plan of action, which is executed with a positive attitude and an expectation of the best in terms of results. A reality thinker who, while seeing the obstacles, can bring to bear on the situation both the power of analysis and the addiction of optimism will be able to overcome any situation.

You are in this world for a divine purpose. What you may have considered as impossible can become possible through God's power. Submit yourself to Him, and He will help you conquer your fears. Fill your heart and mind with love, hope, and faith. The measure of your achievement lies in how you live and serve, not merely in what you are reaching for.

School yourself to look for the good in people, and even in adversity, in order to destroy the forces of negativity. Be of good cheer in all situations. Then, with peace in your mind, love in your heart, and a smile on your face, determine that by the grace of God you will be one of those special people who seek to make every bad situation they face in life good—and good situations even better!

Notes

Chapter 1
1. Raj Chopra, "Expect the Best—and Get It," *Guideposts*, April 1983, pp. 10-12.

Chapter 2
1. *The Nonpareil*, Council Bluffs, Iowa, April 29, 1979.
2. Ibid.
3. Ibid.
4. Ibid.
5. Ibid.
6. *Des Moines Register*, May 9, 1982.

Chapter 4
1. Norman Vincent Peale, *You Can If You Think You Can* (Englewood Cliffs, N. J.: Prentice-Hall, Inc., 1974), pp. 202-203.
2. Dr. James F. Fries, "Aging, Natural Death, and the Compression of Morbidity," *The New England Journal of Medicine*, vol. 303, no. 3, July 17, 1980, pp. 130-35.

Chapter 5
1. Richard H. Schneider, "I Will Not Let You Fail," *Guideposts*, August 1981, pp. 2-7.

Chapter 6
1. Chopra, "Expect the Best," p. 13.
2. Viktor Frankl, *Man's Search for Meaning* (Boston: Beacon Press, 1959).
3. Darrell Sifford, *The Philadelphia Inquirer*, April 24, 1983.
4. Gardner A. McLean, Jr., "Dealing with Teacher Stress," *At Bowling Green*, Bowling Green State University, vol. 11, no. 2, Fall 1981, p. 3.
5. Eugene Jennings, interviewed by John Cunniff, Associated Press, printed in the *Kansas City Star*, January 23, 1983.
6. Ibid.

Chapter 7

1. Chopra, "Expect the Best," p. 14.

2. *Delta Atlas*, Delta, Ohio, November 8, 1983.

3. *The Enterprise*, Swanton, Ohio, November 8, 1983.

4. J. Sterling Livingston, "Pygmalion in Management," *Harvard Business Review*, July-Aug. 1969, p. 81.

5. Ibid., p. 87.

6. Ibid., pp. 81-89.

7. Nancy Dworkin and Yehoash Dworkin, "The Legacy of Pygmalion in the Classroom," *Phi Delta Kappan*, June 1979, pp. 712-15.

Chapter 8

1. Terry Dunnahoo, *Annie Sullivan* (Chicago: Reilly and Lee Books, n.d.), p. 7.

2. Ibid., p. 72.

3. Ibid., pp. 73-4.

4. Ibid., pp. 73-4.

5. Ibid., pp. 95-6.

6. Russell Freedman, *Teenagers Who Made History* (New York: Holiday House, 1961), p. 128.

7. Kathryn Spink, *Miracle of Love* (New York: Harper and Row, 1982).

Chapter 9

1. Frankl, *Man's Search for Meaning*.

2. Norman Cousins, *Anatomy of an Illness* (New York: Bantam Books, 1979), p. 39.